GW01606098

SRI LANKA
A PERSONAL ODYSSEY

Traveller, there is no path. You have to find your own.

SRI LANKA
A PERSONAL ODYSSEY

First Published 1997

Printed in South Korea by
Samhwa Printing Company Ltd.,

Typesetting by Ceylon Printers Limited

Published and distributed by Studio Times Limited,
16/1, Skelton Road, Colombo 5, Sri Lanka.

ISBN 955 - 9236 - 03 -2

For Dodo,
my cherished wife,
touched by all the graces:
truly a prize. . .

Polonnaruwa

One walked between his wife and child,
With measured footfall firm and mild,
And now and then he gravely smiled.
The prudent partner of his blood
Leaned on him, faithful, gentle, good,
Wearing the rose of womanhood.
And in their double love secure,
The little maiden walked demure,
Pacing with downward eyelids pure.
These three made unity so sweet,
My frozen heart began to beat,
Remembering its ancient heat.

\- Alfred Lord Tennyson

Nagrak

Thus in the beginning it was Sri Lanka – The Gem of Gondwana

Sri Lanka is popularly known as the pearl of the Indian Ocean. In geology, we see Sri Lanka as The Gem of Gondwana. In the configuration of Gondwana, Sri Lanka is situated at the central portion of the supercontinent.

- Masaru Yoshida

Preface

"At this blind hour the heart is informed of nature's ruling
That man should be nowhere a more tenacious settler than
Among wry thorns and ruins, yet nurture
A seed of discontent in his ripest ease.
There's a kind of release
And a kind of torment in every goodbye for every man –
And will be, even in the last of his dark departures."

– Cecil Day Lewis

This book may be perceived as a personal lament for a once blessed isle of enchantment, a dirge for the passing of an earthly paradise in which I was fortunate enough to be born, and finally as my kind of epitaph for an Elysium, now defiled, polluted and ravished almost beyond resurrection. If I have succeeded in this simple aim through this testament of pictorial image and complementary text, I shall be content to have fulfilled a challenge of a life-long odyssey before a poet will re-echo :

In the dim wastelands of the orient stands
The wreck of a race so old and vast
That the greatest legend cannot lay hands
On a single fact of its tongueless past.

It has been my good fortune to have travelled on a magic carpet with congenial friends like the late Pat Decker and Herbert Keuneman, and now the young Luxshman Nadaraja – all of whom regard the sky as a tent and appreciated the nuances of landscape in its changing seasons – the colours, the fragrance, the charms, the flavours, and also "the little bit of madness in the people": a people who for centuries sustained large and healthy populations, with advanced agricultural systems in wholesome and friendly environments. Agriculture was the occupation of the majority of the people, and if we are to take the business of culture and development seriously we must accept their belief that agriculture is a culture that binds people and nature together in a Gordian knot, and if you sunder it both will perish. The two are associated with the rhythms of life, of survival, of the essence of production, of creative labour, and the collective and individual dreams of a people. The living world wore an eternal green mantle, and if you removed the green skin the earth would become a graveyard. In my country once was a rich, fecund, vital and enduring human culture, in an abundantly bountiful environment, blessed by two monsoons which replenished the water sources, and a marvellous irrigation system devised by the ancients, with forest-clad hills which ensured a dry weather flow in the lowland valleys. The heritage was indeed rich with a talented people who designed two-storeyed ships, the biggest in Canton harbour, with cargoes of apes, peacocks, gems, elephants and the best cinnamon in the world. The Gal Vihare still stands in eloquent silence – one of the wonders of the world, and a philosophy of religion embodying an ethical code of love, compassion, tolerance and right understanding which suffused an island, compact, small and endowed with enduring values. As Ananda Coomaraswamy summed it all up: "...what we cannot discover at home and in familiar events we cannot discover anywhere. The Holy Land is the land of our experience. All is in all; and if beauty is not apparent to us in the well known, we shall not find it in things that are strange and far-away". *(Rajput Painting,* 1916*)*

What do we find today? A people whose genetic resilience has worn thin, whose children have become links in a consumerist-dominated economic chain, where modes of development dictated by transnational corporations and international financial agencies throttle and imperil indigenous choices. With the New Order in the last two decades appears to have come an unabashed assertion of power, racial superiority and a repudiation of the need for the powerful to obey the law – an end to compassion on the part of the rich for the poor and the weak, and greed as the driving force of this civilization. All geographical and political boundaries are on the point of disappearance or are being forced to disappear as globalization becomes a fact of life in the final triumph of the Market. Economic growth has failed for more than a quarter of the world's people and 89 countries are worse off than they were a decade ago. The world has become more polarized between the rich and the poor, among and within countries, but far more pronounced in the South where the rich have got richer at the expense of the poor. In the past three decades the assets of 358 billionaires exceed the combined incomes of half the world's population of 2.3 billion people! This crazy 'progress' is no option for true development, only a beguiling path to an unknown destination. Neither sustainability nor stability will be served. Far from history ending or having ended, it would seem to be beginning all over again with a fresh cycle of either hope or despair. This surely is a time not for adventure, but for reflection.

Must we follow the profoundly troubled societies of the West, where growth has been achieved with increased crime, drugs, environmental abuse, social debasement and a totally materialistic outlook on life? I have not in this book expressed in pictures the muffled sobs or muted cries of a nation. I have only tried to make the reader observe, think, and realise his heritage, and do what he can to protect it against the forces of evil which have permeated and seeped into our society.

This preface was begun in a garden where every fruit tree grew, every spice, tea, rubber and coconut. I watched the women wash their leech-bitten bloodied feet and go to work in a factory the produce of which is controlled as in all other exports, by a network of cartels. Every roadside bank spouted water, and right here in 1971 I photographed home-made cannon, made with pipes, to fire at the enemy – their own people. We can surely expect more insurrections, more sophisticated and with increased regularity – since it is the only way the trivialised can express defiance of an unjust system which has condemned them to the peripheries of existence. They are the victims of a lop-sided economic growth who are jobless, faceless, voiceless, rootless and futureless. Cultures, community, mutuality, value systems, social fabrics, ecosystems, water storage, seed varieties, biodiversity, forest cover, soil health and coastal conservation have been devalued and deranged. All around are a people ill-nourished, emaciated, indebted, frustrated and too depressed to smile. I cannot resist quoting Prince Charles at the fiftieth anniversary meeting of the Soil Association of Britain in September 1996 : "It is difficult to over-emphasise the significance of what has been unwittingly destroyed in only two generations. We have burdened ourselves and our children with the task of rebuilding what we have destroyed. I fear it may take them most of their lifetime to do so. And the cost both for us and for them will be immense... But the prevailing mood has been that man can dominate Nature and win, and human beings are not only at the top of the food chain, but that manipulation and domination of the natural world is somehow our destiny, even our duty. That I think is where things have gone wrong." (*Island*, 23.9.96)

In my previous book *The Wild, the Free, the Beautiful*, a decade ago, I confessed to having lost every skirmish to keep this island so. I continue to do so – the sanctity of our catchment areas has been violated, elephants fed a sugar-coated pill to desertification, waterfalls to be dehydrated by foreigners who consider their own waterfalls holy, forest cover dwindling with added export crops – all in all an all-encroaching environmental disaster with even the healing rays of the sun becoming lethal. I have now given up all hope and feel much better.

Generations to follow will not see a grasshopper, a butterfly or an elephant. We will have more Kirinde harbours and Samanalawewas, little Hikkaduwas and Negombos in Dambulla, our fish-laden streams, rivers and waterways polluted with insecticides, causing blindness in their users, and children in certain districts will refuse to smile because their teeth are permanently discoloured. Our women will continue to be sold into Middle Eastern slavery so that foreign exchange can flow. The rates of malnutrition and suicide will rise even further, and lower forms of tourism will thrive on increasing poverty. It may be apposite to close this commentary with how E. F. C. Ludowyk, who retained an abiding affection for the land of his birth even in exile, ended his *The Story of Ceylon* (1962) : "The state can be moved to use its powers only by a population aware of what is given and how it can best be changed to meet economic needs and to provide emotional satisfaction. People will grow tired of imagining that they have been eating cake. They will ask for bread and be no longer satisfied with stones." In a Postscript four years later he wrote : "Even if its final words were dismissed as prophecy as yet unfulfilled, they can still, perhaps, remain valid as a general truth, verifiable in the long term if not in the short."

I have communicated the urges that compelled me to undertake this last foray and the pattern of this book is made clear in the table of contents. There is a definite sequence of ideas, or visions beginning with Ceylon as the supposed site of a terrestrial paradise, through its vistas of land, people, history and culture, with emphasis on the variegated heritage, fluctuating fortunes and tides of change, to the finale where I end with my encounter with "the unplumbed, salt - estranging sea" near which the first ten years of my life were spent. The pictures are highly selective and are meant to evoke poetic and haunting glimpses of a beloved land, while the texts from an assembly of writers, far and near, are intended to reinforce, highlight, and underline the purpose of this pictorial exposition. If this book saves an elephant, fosters a tree, or evokes a reverence for what I have revealed, my task has been justified. I have tried to give something back for what I have received – the pleasure of being born in this Eden, once upon a time.

Nihal Fernando

18, Skelton Road, Colombo 5.
25th December, 1996.

Acknowledgments

To Ian Goonetileke, I owe more than the usual expression of thanks for his characteristically generous and self-effacing Introduction which reflects the theme and thrust of my work with his usual verbal felicity. Were it not for his unwavering allegiance to the idea of this book as it developed, and his never-failing advice, encouragement and support from beginning to end, I may have well lost heart. Over nearly half a century, his professional skills and dedication to advancing the cause of learning and scholarship on Sri Lanka have earned him a reputation beyond our shores. An unflurried patience and unerring editorial flair guided me through the numerous currents, shoals and tides of this daunting voyage. His intrinsic modesty prevents me from enlarging further on this debt. The hospitality of his home and the extra pair of eyes that Nayana, his devoted grand-niece provided, were additional boons.

Selvam Canagaratna, a much loved friend for all seasons, who, with unending patience and a generosity beyond understanding, composed the entire text many times over with unfailing cheer.

Neville Weereratne, my old friend from afar, who advised on design and style with his inherent good taste.

Ever gentle Nelun and husband Luxshman Nadaraja for the tolerance and devotion they displayed in the evolution of both format and design.

"One man among a thousand have I found", who was prepared to underwrite the costs of this book, for the sake of an old and valued friendship. He desires anonymity - I was truly blessed in a time of dire need to receive his help.

Dr. Ms. Ratna Handurukande, for the concise and eloquent essay at the beginning of Chapter IV : *Of Buddha and his Message*.

Robert Silva and his wife Chandra for producing a few enchanting verbal interludes where other texts failed me.

Nerina De Silva for verifying the archaeological facts.

Yohan for sorting out the messes I am prone to with a clear head and filial sympathy.

Tony Anghie for a helping hand.

Gamini Punchihewa for his ready responses.

The staff of Studio Times, never found wanting when on call.

The advice and time given graciously by a variety of talented people.

Chaminda, Saman and the staff at Lazergraphic, who showed such enthusiasm for the book, while arranging the final page-making and layouts.

Anu who gifted me with the blessings and joy of a grand-daughter in the course of this venture.

My odyssey enabled me to reinforce and renew my faith in the charm and simplicity of ordinary folk whose friendship, as always, I have valued.

In the final stages the unstinted help of Udaya Wijesoma and Charith Pelpola is greatly appreciated.

Finally, to all those writers, past and present, dead and alive, who shed their light on the paths I chose to travel.

Nihal Fernando

Introduction

"Journeys, like artists, are born and not made. A thousand differing circumstances contribute to them, few of them willed or determined by the will – whatever we may think. They flower spontaneously out of the demands of our natures – and the best of them lead us not only outwards in space, but inwards as well. Travel can be one of the most rewarding forms of introspection."

Lawrence Durrell, poet, novelist, and quintessential interpreter of the spirit of place begins his impressionistic study of the moods and atmospheres of Cyprus when he lived on this then beleaguered island between 1953 and 1956, with this paragraph. I cannot do better than use it as a leitmotif for this Introduction.[1] Who is the true traveller? Someone who beats an arduous path for himself, or someone who discovers a lonely path by himself. There is a difference, and Nihal Fernando is both kinds, but, perhaps, more so of the latter kind. Nihal has taken a lifetime to explore his island, and confesses he would need many more to understand it better, to love it with greater devotion and to uncover yet more unsuspected aspects of its fascinating vitality. He sees clearly and feels deeply, wandering over the country which he has learned to read like the back of his own hand, wherever nature reveals itself to him. For Nihal photography has never lost its interest as a discipline, as a source of pleasure, and a way of life, combined with his ever-active sense of wonderment.

This then is Nihal Fernando's uniquely personal homage to a national heritage he has learned over the long years, to love, to understand and to capture in inexhaustible and unflagging exploration of the photographer's art. These photographs reflect the inspiration of an untiring artist, infected by more than mere enthusiasm and the sensational capacity to use his eyes and the resources of his camera to uncover facets of majestic form and evanescent tone, as well as to reveal the inner grace and hidden beauty of what does not readily unveil itself to the eye of the conventional beholder. "One picture is worth a thousand words" is sadly trite through over-use. Nihal has extended the boundaries and enlarged the dimensions of this perennial truth in ways that those who have traversed the pages of this magnificent book and laid themselves open to the essence of its eloquence will testify to with an enhanced rapture. His mercurial gift for seizing the moment as it passes and his infinite capacity for taking pains are truly remarkable. No limits of patience or physical ardour inhibit his total devotion to the needs of the shutter and the image to be purloined through the twinkling of an exceptional eye.

As Henri Cartier-Bresson, the celebrated French photographer has said: "I may show the whole world in a photograph, but it is the event itself that provokes the organic rhythm of forms ... When I try to photograph an object it is not integrating a bundle of details, but the essence of what has caught **me**, not just the eye. When I photograph a person I must also take in a true reflection of that person's world. Remember the world is as much **inside** the person as **outside**. A balance has to be established between the two, for it is **this** with which I have to communicate. That is why no matter how much I may study my subject, when I click the camera I can only catch what I like to call the fugitive moment. The rest goes into the melting pot."[2]

It is as well therefore to keep one's eyes open. Each image is self-registering, alert and firmly realised. The camera-eye is a mirror-image of the artist's inner vision. Yet this consummate art of fusion arises from an exhilarating familiarity with the forces that pervade nature. Nihal believes that beauty and lyricism lie essentially in the little things of this world, which add up to a whole universe of pictorial metaphor in the end. Each picture is an idea stated with passionate intensity. The eye of the artist looks to discover the inscape of a view or person, the very essence through which it expresses itself. There is a pattern of necessary order in the earth, our only paradise, where man with a sense of the divine creates his own gods. The bliss is evanescent and perishable, but to accept the reality, however fleeting, is to live. This book, from start to finish, takes us into the heart of a country few of us know, back to the land with a dazzling sense of time and place so real we can actually feel the warming sun and smell the rich earth. This striking quality of immediacy and vivid detail is the hallmark of Nihal's artistry. His odyssey possesses the capacity to quicken, disturb, arouse and enliven our humdrum consciousness, because the element of bewitchment is seldom absent. No nauseating, repugnant, ugly, brash and putrescent odours offend the senses in this Arcadia revealed by both a distinctive judgement and a true intuition. In essence this book is an elegiac epitaph to a vanishing Elysium.

1. *Bitter Lemons* (1959) p.15
2. In a conversation with Kamaladevi Chattopadhyay, in her memoirs *Inner Recesses Outer Spaces* (1986) p.315

The survival of animals, birds, marine life and their supporting habitat is no longer a fair contest with the traditional forces of nature. Man in his craving, greed and galloping lust for possession of his world degrades, pollutes and destroys the natural environment. He has no time or thought for the fact that he is hastening the beginnings of his own extinction by the reckless, feckless texture of his materialist fantasies. The numbing monotony of much of modern life is creating in people an unfeeling parody of the machines that were meant to liberate them. The universe appears now to exist only for the pleasure or amusement of man, and he squats on the throne previously reserved for his gods. And so, finally, the world will end not with a bang or a whimper, but in a wasteland of garbage or the common graveyard of a desolate, robotic wilderness.

The tyranny of possession and the culture of cities look poised to engulf what remains of the essential human spirit of individuality, because the metropolis (or megalopolis) stands for materialistic values, pecuniary standards, acquisitiveness and mass-ideas. As Jose Ortega y Gasset put it succinctly in 1930 the mass has advanced from the background of the social stage to the footlights and become the principal character, so that "there are no longer protagonists, there is only the chorus. The mass crushes beneath it everything that is different, everything that is excellent, individual, qualified and select. Anybody who is not like everybody, who does not think like everybody, runs the risk of being eliminated".[3] The ever-increasing preoccupation with things will lead inevitably to the brutalization of the human spirit.

All of us have experienced moments of rare sensation that have lifted us out of the ordinary, the humdrum and the pedestrian purlieus of work-a-day existence. Some of these highs vanish as quickly as they come upon us, others we may be fortunate enough to carry with us our whole lives long. This book contains a kaleidoscope of such shimmering or lasting visions encapsulated for all time, to be recaptured at the flip of a page or a less hurried act of leafing through it for hidden vistas of a reverent insight. This capacity to see anew yet another facet of a well-known artefact, monument, or locale is to be surprised all over again by the freshness and immediacy of what Nihal wishes to reveal. This is not to say that he necessarily finds what he is searching for, yet he has defined his personal directions and announced his agenda without ambiguity. Its structure, scheme and contents are an antidote to the popular and facile notion that modern Western society provides the model that all peoples in the world must follow. The metaphor of 'development' deriving from a purely Western genealogy of history sanctifies global hegemony, robbing peoples of different cultures and civilizations of the right to define or redefine for themselves the form and concepts of their social and ethical life. Popular perceptions of science and its promises of Utopia further erode normal, natural ways of thinking about life and its mysteries.

The world is too much with us and there has never been so much world. Love, duty, principle, vitality, vigour, dignity, grace and warmth of old ways of life are being sucked into a menacing new materialism, where the sheer clutter and false façades of useless things distracts at every turn. Every society under the sun, in greater or lesser degree, suffers an estrangement from their values, a distancing from their cultures, under the sustained assault of a transnational junk culture, which is merely just another cycle of the long process of colonialism, now masquerading as a tantalising World Bank prescription or the compulsive corsage of the global marketplace. The landscapes of the heart are ravished, the territories of the imagination defaced, and the still inviolate regions of the spirit polluted beyond reclamation and repair. In a world that goes so swiftly to the hot dogs, the Burger Kings, and the Kentucky Fried Chickens, one prays that the essential ingredients that make Sri Lanka what it has been and continues to be, will prevail against the forces that threaten to demoralize and undo the faith of age-old values and intelligence. May Pizza Huts never replace wattle and daub fireplaces in *purana gamas* !

Almost four decades ago the distinguished anthropologist Claude Levi-Strauss had the prescience to dwell on what lay in store for us. "I understand how it is that people delight in travel-books and ask only to be misled by them. Such books preserve the illusion of something that no longer exists but yet must be assumed to exist if we are to escape from the appalling indictment that has been piling up against us through twenty thousand years of history. There is nothing to be done about it : civilization is no longer a fragile flower to be carefully preserved and reared with great difficulty here and there in sheltered corners of a territory rich in

3. *The Revolt of the Masses* (1932) Original Spanish, 1930

natural resources: too rich, almost, for there was an element of menace in their very vitality; yet they allowed us to put fresh life and variety into our cultivations. All that is over: humanity has taken to monoculture, once and for all, and is preparing to produce civilization in bulk as if it were sugar-beet. The same dish will be served to us everyday." [4] In some inexplicable way Sri Lanka, both old and new, lives on. In a magical sort of fashion, it is a land of bewildering contrasts where the familiar jostles the recondite, the valleys are as seductive as the hills, and the far becomes the near in the twinkle of an eye. Ananda Kentish Coomaraswamy once observed: "An artist is not a special kind of man, but every man is a special kind of artist." The belief that ordinary every day life, however reduced to simple essentials, can be creative; that imagination is as much a part of the lives of ordinary people and their surroundings as it is of art; that in work and play every man and woman can be their own kind of artist; and that if they were not, they are merely reduced in modern society to puppets, twitched by the fingers of a faceless industry, between drudgery and sensationalism.

Sri Lanka may no longer be what it was, but in essence there is a timeless and unchanging ambience which teases and intrigues at the same time. The wisdom, nonsense, poetry, music, rituals, dances, superstitions, folklore, sorceries, the ceremonies of the unfolding cycle of life and death, the timeless rhythms of the remembered village and the life ways of the peasant remain to stir the unjaded senses. The persistent aura of the past lingers behind the mask of the present, the kernel of soul within the substance of the husk. The more sterilized and stultified we become, the more the nostalgia grows for the simple pleasures and stimulates questions for which the unbridled city has no answers. For most of us nature has an uplifting effect – it is the enticing asylum to which we look in all the years of stress and struggle, in all the moods of anomie, chagrin, angst, or the workings of fate. As I said before, thought for Nihal has a pictorial dimension, animated by light and shade, whatever the nature of the subject or object – sacred or profane. He has the innate ability to give himself up to a particular landscape and the creatures that reside in it, to look at it from as many angles as he can, to wonder about it, and to dwell longingly on it. So also with the devout symbols and monuments of antiquity which lie scattered over the face of this wondrous isle, blessed by the transcendental gift of the teachings of the Buddha. Their timeless beauty and ethereal serenity are revealed in a quickening of our aesthetic senses.

As I write this looking out on a green expanse of fields and woods to which I withdrew five years ago on reaching the Psalmist's span, the sun shines out of a perfectly blue sky, the air is fragrant, the trees glisten, the leaves rustle in the wind, squirrels scurry in the branches, the birds are in full cry, langurs gambol in the distance and the Japanese windbell tinkles in the softest of breezes. Life may be restricted and austere but the renunciations are all in the sphere of action not in that of the heart and mind. So the compensations are compelling. In this rustic bolt-hole, small is always beautiful, and enchantment lies close to the earth. No five-star dreams, however insidious or thrusting, intrude upon long aisles of time in which the joys and sorrows of life reflect the play of past on the present. As one looks back on the years of a vanished past, dispassionately, the realization dawns that the past appears to have receded beyond the horizon of no return. Yet the past assumes securer and comforting forms, and the future can be relished paradoxically through the power of recall. When the ragged banners of daring are furled and the tangled webs of yearning resolved, the precious residue of life has been worth all the lows for the sake of the highs. So Nihal's book unlocks a host of memories of my own restless spirit thirsting to know the enduring contours of my island home in countless miles of unconventional travel from north to south, and west to east in times before the fissures of atavistic violence, civil commotion, and racial strife made such passages hazardous. No more the transports of delight in following the alluring spoors of myth, legend, history and romance off the beaten track: the nights in remote rest houses, homely circuit bungalows, pilgrims' rests, temple *bana maduwas*, village school rooms, the verandahs of little-used churches, bivouacs on lonely beaches, rocky outcrops, or in jungle fastnesses, wherever friends were not happily situated, and, on occasion, the spontaneous hospitality of simple folk. Such travel was the nourishing soil in which one learned to put down roots, and arrive at a lasting sense of personal identity with the silent springs of an age-old culture.

Others, hopefully, will review or engage with this singular peregrination with a greater passion and compassion, keener

4. *Tristes Tropiques* (1959) Translated as: *A World on the Wane* (1962) p.36

insight and a more perceptive eye. For my part these marginal comments arise from the long commitment of an outsider looking in with an increasing load of acute nostalgia, and being invited to participate in this evocatively moveable feast. Having followed the painstaking and exacting nature of this journey of a *kalyana mitra* – a pilgrimage without end because it is always beginning anew in a fresh testament of truth and beauty I wonder whether passion for land and people is as impermanent as falling in love, and, as in this book, ends in a mirage, mirrored in water, where the image mocks at the search or pursuit. But I believe Nihal Fernando has reached and grasped his Holy Grail, following it relentlessly, without rest, from the initial fragmentary idea through the thousands of enchanting images of a giant jigsaw puzzle to its final, persuasive and convincing, pattern of self-discovery. One can only surmise that the pilgrim has found both a passionate pride and an enriching belief in the outcome. The dividing line between success and failure in communicating a deeply held and virtually secret sense of mission is palpitatingly thin. The association, tremulously vicarious, succeeded in seducing me, and I give thanks to Nihal for giving me the opportunity to share a small part of his interior landscape of love and loyalty to the authentic ethos of our island home. That he wished me to write this Introduction is both a gift and a guerdon, so I have been absolutely honest as he has wanted me to be. I hope I have borne the privilege of breaking a lance with the chorus in defence of my protagonist friend to his satisfaction, if not relish. In Homer, Teiresias prophesies to Odysseus that he will suffer a gentle, mysterious end :

"Then a seaborne death
soft as this hand of mist will come upon you
when you are wearied out with ripe old age." [5]

It is also my fervent wish for a friend whose infatuation for our land I share with an undiminished ardour and a continuing concern.

Ian Goonetileke

"Saranam" Oruwela
Athurugiriya.
07 May, 1996.

POSTSCRIPT

My *Introduction* was written in the early part of last year, and Nihal Fernando's caravan has taken longer than envisaged to arrive at its destination. I have now seen all the pictures and texts, and read his Preface. So mood, space and *raison d'etre* compel me to a necessary *Postscript* in the dawn of another year. This book is a moving plea on behalf of a self-reliant and self-respecting rural peasantry whose ingrained cultural and social institutions, traditional mores and conventions of thought and action have been threatened by development models moored in consumerism and materialist ideologies. The political, socio-economic and spiritual-cultural strands of a development process vital for the equitable distribution of the social product and the national wealth among all classes in a plural society have yet to be spelled out and synthesised into a recognisable and viable frame of understanding and concern to secure the objectives of a socialist democracy that all governments have declared as their political creed since Independence. Too often have resounding platitudes masqueraded as profound truths, phantoms been mistaken for realities, and shadows metamorphosed into substance.

Environmental degradation, bio-piracy, the squandering of the diminishing ecological base, an insensibility to social injustice, islands of pomp and power amidst widening swamps of deprivation only serve to fertilise tomorrow's hazards. The hypnotic fixation on instant bliss, the desires of the moment, and quick returns hasten day-after-tomorrow's resentment and violence. To plunder the present landscape is to pillage the remaining vestiges of a dwindling heritage for the children yet to be born. It is the cardinal message of **Sri Lanka, A Personal Odyssey**, the truly candid and strenuous soul-searching of a stricken conscience in a crumbling Eden.

I. G.
05 January 1997

5. *The Odyssey* A new translation by Robert Fitzgerald (1961)

Contents

the earth was without form and void

\- Genesis

I. Creation

The First Book of Moses
called
GENESIS

CHAPTER I
In the beginning God created the heaven and the earth.
2 And the earth was without form, and void; and darkness was upon the face of the deep.

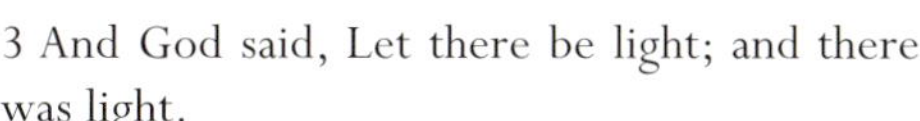

3 And God said, Let there be light; and there
was light.
4 And God saw the light, that *it was* good: and
God divided the light from the darkness.
5 And God called the light Day, and the darkness he called Night. And the evening and the
morning were the first day.

And the Spirit of God moved upon the face of the waters.

6 And God said, Let there be a firmament in the
midst of the waters, and let it divide the waters
from the waters.
7 And God made the firmament, and divided
the waters which *were* under the firmament from
the waters which *were* above the firmament: and
it was so.
8 And God called the firmament Heaven. And
the evening and the morning were the second
day.

9 And God said, Let the waters under the heaven
be gathered together unto one place, and let the
dry *land* appear: and it was so.
10 And God called the dry *land* Earth; and the
gathering together of the waters called he Seas:
and God saw that *it was* good.
11 And God said, Let the earth bring forth grass,
the herb yielding seed, *and* the fruit tree yielding fruit after his kind, whose seed *is* in itself,
upon the earth: and it was so.
12 And the earth brought forth grass, *and* herb
yielding seed after his kind, and the tree yielding fruit, whose seed *was* in itself, after his kind:
and God saw that *it was* good.
13 And the evening and the morning were the
third day.

14 And God said, Let there be lights in the firmament of the heaven to divide the day from
the night; and let them be for signs, and for seasons, and for days, and years:

15 And let them be for lights in the firmament
of the heaven to give light upon the earth: and it
was so.
16 And God made two great lights; the greater
light to rule the day, and the lesser light to rule
the night: *He made* the stars also.
17 And God set them in the firmament of the
heaven to give light upon the earth,
18 And to rule over the day and over the night,
and to divide the light from the darkness: and
God saw that it was good.
19 And the evening and the morning were the
fourth day.

20. And God said, Let the waters bring forth
abundantly the moving creature that hath life,
and fowl *that* may fly above the earth in the open
firmament of heaven.
21 And God created great whales, and every living creature that moveth, which the waters
brought forth abundantly, after their kind, and
every winged fowl after his kind: and God saw
that it *was* good.

22 And God blessed them, saying, Be fruitful,
and multiply, and fill the waters in the seas, and
let fowl multiply in the earth.
23 And the evening and the morning were the
fifth day.

24 And God said, Let the earth bring forth the
living creature after his kind, cattle, and creeping thing, and beast of the earth after his kind:
and it was so.

25 And God made the beast of the earth after
his kind, and cattle after their kind, and every
thing that creepeth upon the earth after his kind:
and God saw that it was good.

26 And God said, Let us make man in our image, after our likeness: and let them have dominion over the fish of the sea, and over the fowl
of the air, and over the cattle, and over all the
earth, and over every creeping thing that
creepeth upon the earth.
27 So God created man in his own image, in the
image of God created he him; male and female
created he them.

28 And God blessed them, and God said unto
them, "Be fruitful and multiply, and fill the earth
and subdue it; and have dominion over the fish of
the sea and over the birds of the air and over
every living thing that move upon the earth."
29 And God said, "Behold, I have given you
every herb bearing seed, which *is* upon the face
of all the earth, and every tree, in the which *is* the
fruit of a tree yielding seed to you it shall be for
meat.
30 And to every beast of the earth, and to every
fowl of the air, and to every thing that creepeth
upon the earth, wherein *there is* life, *I have given*
every green herb for meat": and it was so.
31 And God saw every thing that he had made,
and, behold, *it was* very good. And the evening
and the morning were the sixth day.

CHAPTER 2

THUS the heavens and the earth were
finished, and all the host of them.
2 And on the seventh day, God ended his work
which he had made; and he rested on the seventh
day, from all his work which he had made.
3 And God blessed the seventh day, and sanctified it: because that in it he had rested from all his

5 And every plant of the field before it was in
the earth, and every herb of the field before it
grew: for the Lord God had not caused it to rain
upon the earth, and *there was* not a man to till the
ground.
6 But there went up a mist from the earth, and
watered the whole face of the ground.

4 These are the generations of the heavens and
of the earth when they were created, in the day
that the Lord God made the earth and the
heavens,

7 And the Lord God formed man of the dust of
the ground, and breathed into his nostrils the
breath of life and man became a living soul.
8 And the Lord God planted a garden eastward
in Eden; and there he put the man whom he had
formed.

9 And out of the ground made the Lord God to
grow every tree that is pleasant to the sight, and
good for food; the tree of life also in the midst of
the garden, and the tree of knowledge of good
and evil.
10 And a river went out of Eden to water the
garden and from thence it was parted, and became
into four heads.

II. A good land

Polonnaruwa

A land of brooks, of water,
of fountains and springs,
Flowing forth in valleys and hills
... in which you will lack nothing.
- Deuteronomy

When gliding noiselessly in a canoe, nothing can be more striking than the sensation caused by turning unexpectedly into one of those quiet and unfrequented openings, where dense foliage lines each side and almost meets above the water. The trees are covered with birds of gorgeous plumage; pea-fowl sun themselves on the branches, and snowy egrets and azure kingfishers station themselves lower down to watch the fish, which frequent these undisturbed pools in prodigious numbers. The silence and stillness of these places is quite remarkable; the mournful cry of the water-fowl is heard from an incredible distance; and the splash of a crocodile as he plunges into the stream, or the surprise of a deer when, disturbed at his morning draught he

"Stamps with all his hoofs together,
Listens with one foot uplifted."

- Sir James Emerson Tennent, *Ceylon*, 1860

Hambegamuwa

Negombo

CREDO

Mountains, and woods, and the winds that
 blow over them;
Meadows, and downs, and the wild flowers
 that cover them;
Rocks, and ravines, and the jungles that
 smother them;
All these I love with a love that possesseth me,
 But more than all of these I worship thee.

Sea, and the shore, and shells the gods
 squander there;
Corals, and pools, and wild things that wander
 there;
Silence, and caves, and the thoughts that men
 ponder there;
All these I love with a love that enchanteth me,
But deeper in my depths springs love for thee.

- John Still,
The Jungle Tide, 1930

Around us rose the bastions of encircling hills clothed in forest which concealed a vast wealth of animal life: beyond these was a second range; and behind them a third; and so range beyond range, until finally fuliginous contours billowed against a crimson sky seeming to belong more to cloud-land than to earth. The sunset flared like a beacon scattering smoky flocculi. The dark crept to the whispering of cool night winds, the gemmed sky canopied the sleep of those solitudes, and the cold and comfortless moon looked down. Into our hearts crept a quiet, old as earth.

- R.L.Spittel, *Wild Ceylon*, 1945.

An introduction to Sri Lanka

I love her hills; I love her winding streams;
I love her glades and grass and fern:
My kin are there; and from afar my dreams
Are of her glory once again.
That land is Lanka, fairest isle of all,
Whose hills the clouds do hug and kiss:
That land is Lanka, at whose sacred call
Our hearts do stir with pride and bliss.
There's a land I know where the winds do
softly blow...

- J. Vijayatunga

Mawanella

Anuradhapura

Panahaduwa

When the sun rises, I go to work,
When the sun goes down, I take my rest,
I dig the well from which I drink,
I farm the soil that yields my food,
I share creation, Kings can do no more.

\- Ancient Chinese Poem, 2500 B.C.

Hettipola

Cooking rice and eating and drinking as we fancy,
Feeding with grass the two bulls and giving
them water,
In the cattle-shed tonight taking it easy and
delaying,
At two in the morning, comrade, let us set out
from here.

Because of poverty the bulls are bound and
driven;
Exhausted we for want of food both night and
day;
All manner of trouble giving the bulls we
drive them;
For this misery now the gods will look with
favour!

\- tr. George Keyt,
"A Carter's Song" *Poetry from the Sinhalese*, 1938,
verses 5 & 6.

Wattegama

The real Ceylon, as I see it, is found in the pale-green paddy-field with its threshing-floor upraised, while the thatched huts of the peasantry cluster under the coconut-trees on the high ground: in the white-robed worshippers on *poya* night bearing offerings to some little village temple; in the wastes of the Wanni; or on the sea-shore when the fishing-nets are hauled in, alive with struggling silvery fishes. Perhaps the most typical picture of all is the fragile watch-hut in a small *chena*, where by day and night man defends against the birds of the air and the beasts of the field his meagre crop of *Kurakkan*, upon which he and his skinny family are dependent, if something more than bare existence is to be enjoyed.

\- C. Brooke Elliott, *The Real Ceylon*, 1938.

From the ricefields
Straighten the back bent all day to the ground
Put down the sheaf you have in your hands,
Pull off the towel you have tied round your head.
The gods be praised, let's get out of the mud!
- Ashley Halpe,
Homing and other poems, 1993.

Akurana

Wasgamuwa

Along the river bank, below God's Hill, the trees looked as if they were covered with powder puffs; and it was only when we drew near that they resolved themselves into painted storks with delicate pink, white, and greeny-black plumage, grey herons and parson cranes - these properly called white-necked storks, there being no cranes in Ceylon. The colony seemed to be confined to this spot, where about half-a-dozen low trees were laden with their stick nests. These birds were extra-ordinarily tame, and except for one or two did not trouble to fly away at our approach, showing that here, at least, although it is not a sanctuary, they were not harassed overmuch by man.

- D. J. G. Hennessy, *Green Aisles*, 1949.

◄ *Ehetuwewa*

I can see it to this day, that radiant panorama, that wilderness of rich color, that incomparable dissolving-view of harmonious tints, and lithe half-covered forms, and beautiful brown faces, and gracious and graceful gestures and attitudes and movements, free unstudied, barren of stiffness and restraint.

- Mark Twain, *Following the Equator*, 1900.

Ehetuwewa

Round these tanks in ancient times, as still in many places in Ceylon, would cluster the fields and houses of the village. Village and tank were almost synonymous. For the cultivator the rhythm of life would be set by the seasonal work in the rice-fields. Besides there were cattle to feed, and some hunting to be done for at hand was the jungle. The village had its various craftsmen who made it self-sufficient, and it had its council of elders to regulate its affairs and to settle disputes. Important among the tasks of the community was the duty of keeping embankment and channel in repair, and of building new works when need arose. This labour undertaken by the community for its own benefit becomes in the course of time the institution of *Rajakariya*, or work performed for the king. The builders of tanks like Mahasen and Parakkama Bahu I could put their vast schemes into effect only because the labour which went into them was service rendered by the community. Of course such service could be either voluntarily performed or forcibly exacted. It is a well known fatality of institutions that the best in them is subject to decay and corruption, and it may be that some of the labour of the community needed for construction, of tank and channel was arbitrarily demanded and tyrannously enforced in later times. But one can see that the prosperity, nay the survival, of these village communities, each of them grouped round a tank depended on the voluntary labour of the whole unit. As long as the community remained intact, the water on which it depended could provide it with the means for survival. Equally true is the reflection that as long as the system of irrigation works remained intact, the community could survive. As long as the life-giving water was conserved in the tank, or the channel undamaged which brought it from its further source, the village prospered and could maintain, in spite of the variability of seasons of drought and rain, its simple standards of decent well-being.

- E. F. C. Ludowyk,
The Footprint of the Buddha, 1958.

Its unchanging tropical loveliness, the mysteriousness of its past, the soft yet excitable character of its people, its prevalence of strange animals, birds and flowers all combined to make life in Ceylon an experience now unequalled anywhere.

- Vinton Liddell Pickens, *Serendipity*, 1964

Gal Oya

In a shallow bay of that tank there stood a grove of dead trees whose roots had been drowned when the tank was restored twenty years before, and now their bark had all peeled off and they were bleached white by the sun. One does not see trees like that in the forest, for their wood is devoured by termites before they have been very long dead. Scores of black divers used to stay for an hour at a time with wings outstretched like coats of arms, while they sat on the branches of the dead trees and dried themselves; and egrets nested there, and dropped their precious white plumes into the water where young crocodiles waited for the young birds to learn to fly.

- John Still,
The Jungle Tide, 1930.

Anuradhapura

Let them come and see men and women and children who know how to live, whose joy of life has not yet been killed by those who claimed to teach other nations how to live.

- Chinua Achebe

Hettipola

Negombo

Deniyaya

Negombo

Time in the course of a thousand or two thousand years has made both the ruined tank against which one nudges in the jungle, and those which restored still conserve the volume of water they used to impound, so much a part of the natural landscape that it is hard to think of them now as the work of men and women. They lie so naturally in the fold of the land, and resemble lakes in pleasant hollows with grassy and treed banks that the mind sees them as existing from the beginning of time. To one who has wandered on their banks and gazed over their sheets of water, it would seem that the serenity they have inherited enforces something more than a philosophical commonplace, and that the extraordinary feeling of calm they seem to bestow on the beholder mirrors in some way one of the contemplative virtues the Buddha preached.

These people who toiled in the mud of the rice-fields, working with their hands on the bund and on the moulding of earth, were people physically linked with the earth in the way all early agricultural communities have been. To call them 'primitive' would be unfortunate, because that word might imply a value judgement entered against them. Round them, not quite tamed or subservient, was the earth they knew, manifesting itself through various presences on knoll, river, lake, hill and grove. These were the gods of the earth to whom offerings were made and whose aid was sought in every activity of the community. The *Yakkhas* of the later chronicles were these earth-gods worshipped by the inhabitants of these village communities of ancient Ceylon. Not a tank but had its own water-spirit, not a grove but had its guardian god. Reference has already been made to tutelary deities which the 'Aryan' invaders must have known in their home on the mainland. The cults of some of these would have been brought over and have been acclimatized in the new island home.

- E. F. C. Ludowyk,
The Footprint of the Buddha, 1958.

◂*Kahandamodera*

Ukuwela
Balaluwewa

Those coco-palms not fair in the woods,
But singly seen and seen afar,-
When sunlight pours its yellow floods,
A column and its crown a star!

- J. Ferguson,
Ceylon in 1893.

They have no want of Fish, and those good ones too. All little Rivers and Streams running thro the Valleys are full of small Fish, but the Boys and others wanting somewhat to eat with their Rice do, continually catch them before they come to maturity: and all their Ponds are full of them, which in dry weather drying up, the people catch multitudes of them in this manner. They have a kind of a Basket made of small Sticks so close that Fish cannot get thro; it is broad at bottom and narrow at top, like a funnel, the hole big enough for a man to thrust his Arm in, wide at the mouth about two or three foot; these baskets they jobb down, and the ends stick in the mud, which often happen upon a Fish; when they do, they feel it by the Fish beating itself against the sides. Then they put in their hands and take them out. And rieve a Rattan thro their gills, and so let them drag after them. One end of this Rattan is stuck in the fisher's girdle, and the other knotted, that the fish should not slip off: which when it is full, he discharges himself of them.

- Robert Knox,
An Historical Relation Of the Island Ceylon, 1681.

Galgamuwa
Balaluwewa

That Light

The light in Ceylon that was life to me
was death to me, too - for to live
in a diamond's intensity
is the lonely lyceum of corpses:
a bird made diaphanous
suddenly, a spider webbing the sky, and then
gone.

Stung by the light of those islands,
I keep circumspect always,
as though a beam of that faraway
honey might turn me to ash in a moment.

More remote than the puma,
I moved out of range, knowing nobody,
dreading the occipital light of a paradise
that might one day explode in my brain.
(Light, falling on black, pierces more than the
clothing –
it cuts through the wearer's decorum: I struggle
to live every day in an aura of nakedness, now.)

Those never so wholly alone
in themselves, will not understand this, or
come closer;
nor so lost as I seemed to be then,
a carbonized number at midnight.

There is left us the bread and the light.

The soul's light, and the light of the kitchen,
night light and the light of the morning,
light under the sheets of a dream.
Suckld by light,
I live as I must
in my destiny's ruthless lucidity,
between the luminous and the desperate halves,
disowned
by two kingdoms which never were mine.
The net cords that shake in the light
keep their clear intimation of ocean.

The sheer light of time is here with us still,
midday in its consummate tower.

All turns to darkness, it seems to me now.

- Pablo Neruda,
A New Decade : Poems 1958 - 1967 (1969)

Mawanella

Birds (Extracts)

Grey, red-hued
two ash-doves
peck grain in my yard,
I am lonely.

I am better than you
at sucking honey
soft, colourful, butterfly.

You may fly
high
over the mountain, hawk,
but you cannot soar
as high as my thoughts.

Where does the curlew go shrieking?
My mind has nowhere to go to like that.

The king-fisher threw me a feather
flying by.
She of the shining form
went
leaving nothing behind.

Thick silence,
bird-song
a black stain
on a white canopied sky.

In a silence that holds not a sound
but bird-song
they are eager to sing.
The intense silence
picks up their cries.

The sound of a violin
in a still hall
cuts through
stands out
like the body of a young girl.
Bird song here
is like that.

\- G. B. Senanayake,
tr. Ranjini Obeyesekere. *An Anthology of Modern Writing from Sri Lanka* (1981) p.43

Udawalawe

Kurunegala

Negombo

Water

Nothing is lovelier than moving water,
The diamond element, innumerable jewel,
Brittle and splintering under the sharp sun,
Yet softer than doves' feathers, and more smooth
Than down of swan.

Nothing is lovelier than water lying still,
When the Moon takes that stillness for her glass.
- Gerald Bullett, *Poems in Pencil*, 1937.

What would the world be, once bereft
Of wet and of wildness? Let them be left,
Oh let them be left, wildness and wet;
Long live the weeds and wilderness yet.
- Gavin Maxwell, 1968.

Galgamuwa

… rushing through ravines and glens, and falling over precipitous rocks in the depths of wooded valleys, they exhibit a succession of rapids, cataracts, and torrents, unsurpassed in magnificence and beauty. On reaching the plains, the boldness of their march and the graceful outline of their sweep are indicative of the little obstruction opposed by the sandy and porous soil through which they flow.

- Sir John Emerson Tennent, *Ceylon*, 1860.

Knuckles

Bulutota

Where each old poetic mountain
Inspiration breathed around:
Every shade and hallowed fountain
Murmured deep a solemn sound.
- Thomas Gray

Slowly, silently, now the moon
Walks the night in her silver shoon.
- Walter de La Mare

Knuckles

Anuradhapura

The pastures of the wilderness drip, the hills gird themselves with joy, the meadows clothe themselves with flocks, the valleys deck themselves with grain, they shout and sing together for joy.
- *Psalm 65*: Verses 12-13, paraphrase.

And in the left foreground the small white stupa, so simple and so chaste, glittering in the sun's lengthening rays; the scent from its flower-altars penetrating the ambient air. A little to the right of it, on the other side of the meticulously-swept yard, the white-walled shrine-room and the bana-mandalaya or preaching hall. This was the village temple. There; focussed in the heart of its heart-land of green-gold, growing paddy. Was it artist or philosopher who had selected the site, already designed by Nature? And laid it out in such exquisite euphony?
- Maureen Seneviratne

Mawanella
Ampara

There is something so extravagantly romantic in those sequestered spots, that they inspire the mind with unusual pleasure. A traveller may there behold her unblemished features and undisguised charms; and a person who is fond of meditation, and recollection of past events, may here enjoy all the luxury of solitude. Every discordant passion is lulled to rest: the most complacent benevolence warms the soul; and the mind triumphs in unbounded freedom amidst peaceful tranquility. The wildness and luxuriance, and sublimity and beauty, of the scenes probably equal any combination which rural grandeur can display. Whilst employed in contemplating them, the power of utterance is lost in silent admiration, and the eye wanders with astonishment and rapture from the rocky brow of the lofty mountain to the rich pastures of the fertile valley.

- Rev. James Cordiner,
A Description of Ceylon, 1807.

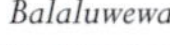

Balaluwewa

In the account I have given of the gems of the island, I did not mention the manner in which they are sought for. The mode is so simple, that it hardly deserves the name of an art. It is only in alluvial ground, it has been remarked, that these scarce and beautiful minerals have yet been discovered in Ceylon. Where there is a probability of finding them, pits are sunk from three to twenty feet deep; the coarse sand and gravel through which they are generally disseminated, is collected and carried in baskets to an adjoining stream, where it is well washed; the lighter particles are got rid of by a rotary motion given to the basket in the operation; and the residue, still wet, is transferred to shallow baskets for careful examination. Not only gems, the great object of the search, are collected, but every stone that has the least chance of finding a purchaser in the market. Like mining in general, the occupation of searching for gems is a very precarious one: in Ceylon it cannot be considered a profitable pursuit; and there is good reason to believe that the individuals engaged in it, who are not very numerous, and chiefly moormen, would be better employed in cultivating the ground that they ransack.

- John Davy,
An account of the interior of Ceylon, 1821.

Of commodities

For in certain places where they are known to be, are sharp Poles set up fixed in the ground, signifying, that none upon pain of being stuck and impaled upon those Poles, presume so much as to go that way. Also there are certain Rivers, out of which it is generally reported they do take Rubies and Sapphires for the King's use, and Cats eyes. And I have seen several pretty coloured stones, some as big as Cherry-stones, some as Buttons, and transparent, but understood not what they were. Rubies and Sapphires I my self have seen here.

- Robert Knox, 1681.

Gilimale

Pelmadulla

Nuwara Eliya Lake, 1960

Our ecological heritage - on to the 21st century

Life arose from the primordial surging waters of the seas. Amidst the breathless spectacle of volcanic eruptions, casting cathedrals of light across the heavens, lowly creatures or beings crept on to the wave bashed, foam covered cliffs rising from the seas.

Water, the life blood of all forms of life; together with the biomass recycling carbon dioxide into oxygen for creatures low and almighty; reigns supreme in the evolutionary and survival process.

Our nostalgia goes back to an earlier era of the present century - when the mists drifted gracefully over the green hills and forests of our land - mists that carried our sighs which lingered with the simmering dew.

Alas, uncontrolled population growth, and the 'March of Folly' – political expediency coupled with bureaucratic chicanery - has fractured a fragile ecological environment.

Our life blood, water and oxygen, our hydro power and rational settlement projects are being spiked at their very source.

As we march into the 21st. century; picture a glorious cloud decked morn, the sun splashing the sky with rainbow hues, and the mountains in their blazing rapture, crying out, the dawn is here, the dawn is here! But a man may say that all his thoughts are centred on that dreadful dawn when man may cry – 'O scorching sun, O cloudless sky, my mountains are but barren rocks!'

By halting this 'March of Folly' and with judicious husbanding and rational management of our population and ecological resources, could we not usher in material adequacy coupled with environmental tranquility?

This is my prayer for the 21st. century – I will not be there, but others will!

- W. R. H. Perera, 1996.

The sedge is withered from the lake,
And no birds sing.

- John Keats.

Nuwara Eliya, 1960

Nuwara Eliya, 1960

Jungle clearance Ceylon

In a manmade lake at first light
Cruising between the tops of bleached
Skeleton trees we waited for elephant
Coming to drink. They never came
But, focussing in, on each bare branch
Of the bonewhite trees we marked a pelican
Frozen to fossil, looking down
Its beak in contempt of human beings
Who had drowned a valley to found a town –
Power and water for human beings
In the thick of the bush. In the thin of the trees
The pelican perched as though in a glass
Case where the wind could never blow
Nor elephant come to drink nor human
Beings presume in the grey dawn
To press a button or throw a switch
To slap the west on the back of the east
In spite of archaic and absent elephant
In spite of archaic and present pelican
In spite of themselves as human beings.

- Louis MacNeice, *Solstices*, 1961.

Handapanagala

III. A strange world

Horton Plains

It was a strange world, a world of bare and brutal facts, of superstition and grotesque imagination; a world of trees and the perpetual twilight of their shade; a world of hunger and of fear and devils, where a man was helpless before the unseen and unintelligible powers surrounding him.

- Leonard Woolf, *The Village in the Jungle*, 1913

In some parts of Ceylon, where forests are rapidly becoming a memory to the old and a tradition to the young, almost every village has somewhere within its borders a grove, a little bit of woodland left uncut and uncleared: it may be only a few perches in area, but it is the home of a god. No image is there, but in a tiny room is kept some garment, or an ornament, or a spear or sword, something that is the god's own property, and which his priest holds or wears when he becomes inspired and dances or utters prophecies in the god's name. The priest is the god for the time being, and nothing more utterly different from Buddhism could be devised; yet the people who worship, and the men who rank as priests, all profess and call themselves Buddhists, and are described as such in the census returns. I suspect these temples in groves to be closely allied to the wood-god worship of the forest, for their homes are still woods, if only a few yards square.

- John Still, *The Jungle Tide*, 1930

Hettipola Tree Shrine

Magul Maha Vihara - Yala

I think the people of the jungle take these gods more seriously than they do Buddhism. They seem to attach more value to the power of the older gods to assist them in calamity; and they value oaths taken in their presence so highly that a man will often challenge his enemy to make oath in a dewale.

- John Still, *The Jungle Tide*, 1930

Hill Country

Hill Country

Kurunegala Tree Shrine

Yala

Kalawewa

Once – and once only; in that village of which I have spoken –lying awake in my bed in that bitterest dark before the dawn I heard from the jungle three wide-spaced eerie cries ringing into the cold black sky. I had been told of a weird form of exorcism which calls for the exorcist to lay himself all night in an open grave in the jackal-haunted corner of a wilderness.

- Herbert Keuneman,
unpublished ms. circa 1973.

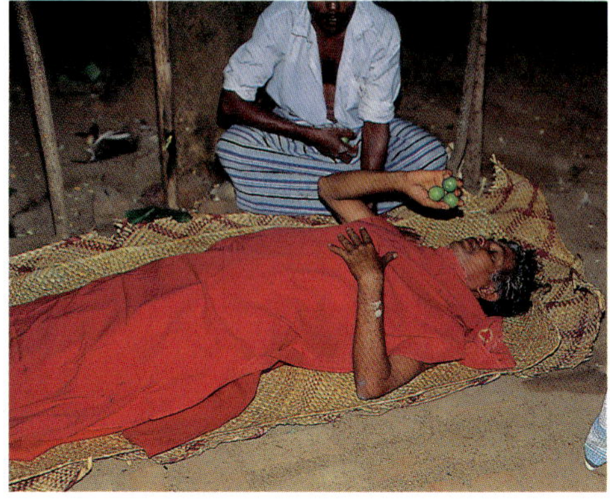

Ehetuwewa

The Ceremony of "Passing through Fire", or "Walking over Flowers". - There is a curious ceremony, not generally known, that obtains in Puttalam and some other parts of this district at certain seasons of the year, which, I believe, has not been mentioned in any report to Government, and which is nevertheless well worthy of record. It is the ceremony of passing through the fire, or walking over flowers as it is euphemistically called in Tamil, and is in all probability the very same barbarous rite that was practised about 2,600 years ago by Ahaz, the son of Jotham, King of Judah, and by the idolatrous kings of Israel before him, who passed their children through the fire to Moloch according to the abomination of the heathen. The modern ceremony (as was probably the ancient one) is of Hindu origin, and is practised chiefly, I believe, in Southern India. In this part of Ceylon it is held in many villages of the Puttalam District, especially at Mundel and at Udapankarre, 15 and 20 miles south of the Puttalam salt pans. Among the Hindus, it is the closing ceremony of the fast which commemorates the trials of the virgin queen. "Tropa Devi", who was married to the five sons of the king of Pandu (Madura) and whose history is, I believe, recorded in the Mahabharata. Though married to these five brothers, she still remained a virgin, and through her chastity and virtue became possessed of supernatural powers. This immaculate princess had made a vow not to fasten up her hair, until she could do so standing on the head of King Turiyodanan, who had deprived her husbands of their kingdom, and had driven them and her into exile into the forest. By miraculous powers she had acquired and vanquished this king, cut off his head, and standing on it fastened up her hair. The kingdom was of course restored to the sons of Pandu. The fast lasts eighteen days, and begins about the end of June. It is inaugurated by hoisting a flag opposite the temple of Tropa Devi, and from that day the *kapurala* or priest reads a book called the Pataran or Pataranga Jataka to the assembled multitude. The persons who intend to take part in the concluding ceremony live during the whole fast on vegetable food.-

Frank Modder,
Manual of the Puttalam District, 1908

Udappu
Udappu - Fire Walking

Wasgamuwa

Dambulla

The jungle villagers, although theoretically of the Buddhist religion, were in practice, like their ancestors the Veddas, worshippers of the jungle gods. Among the dim arcades and leafy aisles of the forest dwell the ageless gods, shy beings upon whose face no man has looked. So everywhere in the jungle we came upon their rude altars; perhaps a tripod of rough sticks with a bunch of leaves offered upon it, or only a tuft of foliage placed against a tree with earnest prayers, or a less primitive shrine consisting of an empty tin or box in which were a flickering light and a few leaves for altar fire and sacrifice. Not only do these folk worship gods but, like the Veddas, they fear and propitiate demons. The root of their worship is fear - fear of the unknown and of the weird sounds and flitting shadows.

- D. J. G. Hennessy,
Green Aisles, 1949.

Negombo

On Saturday morning after Mass, there used to be enacted, in some Paskus, the scene of the devils being let loose. The village boys blacken their faces and run amok, looting vendors and playing havoc among the people. Then comes Lucifer, heralded by the sound of loud gongs, and all the devils concentrate into one of the side stages. Here Lucifer questions them about their doings and the devils begin to reveal all the clandestine affairs and private intrigues of the village folk, each devil confessing to his having been responsible for a certain number of evils. The boys took this opportunity of revealing village gossip and scandal, and altercations of a serious sort often resulted. On account of this, the scene with Lucifer and the devils was banned from Passion Plays.

- E. R. Sarachchandra,
The Folk Drama of Ceylon, 2nd ed. 1966

Oruwela

Kataragama

Two dramatic interludes that occur in the ceremony known as a Gam Maduva, are the *Amba Vidamana*, the Shooting of the Mango, and *Rãma Märima*, the Killing of Rãma. The Gam Maduva is a collective ritual performed to propitiate several deities, and generally intended to ward off evil and bring prosperity to the crops. The ceremonies usually begin after the harvesting, when the first portion of paddy, collected from every household, is cooked, and offered at the altars of the various gods, like Dädimunda, Kataragama, Saman, Vibhisana, and, of course the goddess Pattini. This initial ritual is known as *murutän pidima*, or Offering New Rice. Then follows the set of ceremonies associated with the worship of Pattini (*Pattini Bhäge*). The priest brings the ornaments of Pattini from the *devälaya*, and places them on the main altar (*torana*). This is followed by group dancing, in which the chief priest as well as attendant dancers take part. The dancing ends with the priest "exhibiting the anklets', that is, he carries the anklets in his trembling hands and walks from altar to altar in a trance, and finally deposits them in the main altar. The *Pattini Bhäge* is followed by a dance called *Telme Nätima*, or the Oil Service. A stand made of the pith of the banana tree (*kehel bada*) and tender coconut leaves (*gokkola*) is placed in the middle of the ring. It is lit up with torches (*vilakku*), and dancing goes on round it.

- E. R. Sarachchandra,
The Folk Drama of Ceylon, 2nd ed., 1966.

Kalawewa

The world of the Sri Lankan villager is full of malevolent spirits and hungry ghosts who live in a parallel world and live an organised life as humans do. They have a kingdom ruled by King Vesamuni, and Mahasona is the chief of sixty thousand demons. Spirits are said to have regular pandemoniums on saturdays and wednesdays which are the days on which the devale priests have their thevave (ritual homage) to their gods. At these meetings called 'yakshasamagamas' each demon chief gives an account of those under him; after which they all indulge in dancing, singing, playing musical instruments, and in the display of exploits of skill and dexterity.

- Dandris de Silva Gooneratne,
"On demonology and witchcraft in Ceylon",
J.R.A.S.C.B. 4 (13) 1865-6.

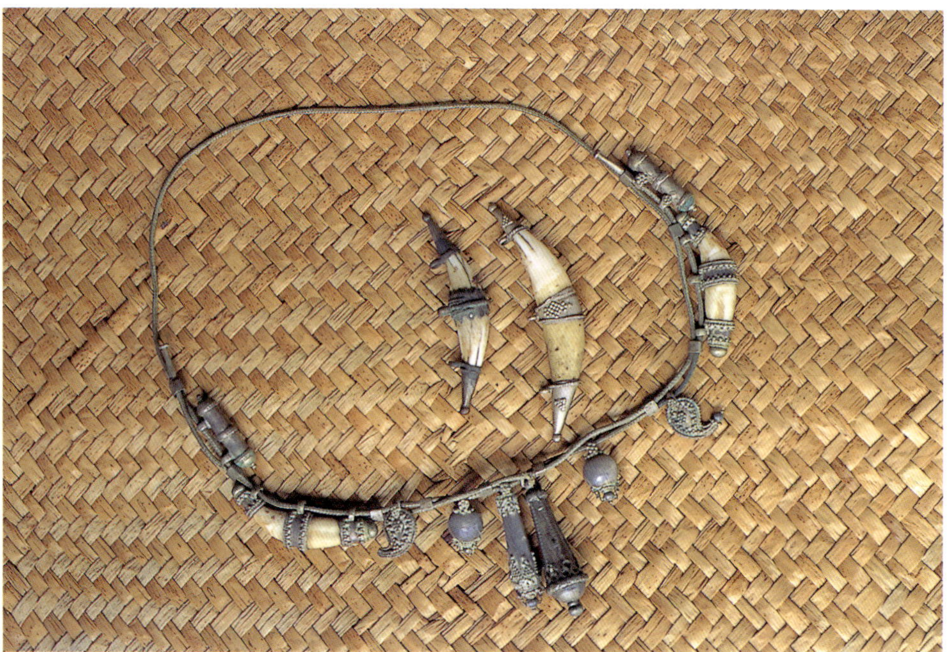

Koggala Folk Art Museum

The term "Yantra" is also loosely applied to certain objects worn on the person such as gems, leopard teeth, (amulets), ornaments, certain metals, and lockets containing oils (talismans). These objects are said to possess intrinsic magical powers which are sometimes amplified with incantations. The term is also applied to auspicious symbols which are used as good luck charms. Some yantras are inscribed on thin strips of metal or strips of palm leaf and worn in lockets. Both the palm leaf and the metal strip are substances born of the creative forces of the earth, and therefore the materials are treated with respect, and the rules prescribed for their preparation carefully followed.

\- L. S. D. Peiris, 1996.

Ehetuwewa

But wild beasts of the desert shall lie there; and their houses shall be full of doleful creatures; and owls shall dwell there, and satyrs shall dance there. And the wild beasts of the islands shall cry in their desolate houses, and dragons in their pleasant palaces; and her time is near to come, and her days shall not be prolonged.

- *Isaiah*, Ch. 13, verses 21-22

Wasgamuwa

Haldumulla
Yala

Fear in the Forest

Alone upon a wooded hill I lay,
Beneath a pale blue sky, where swifts did fly,
And listened while the voices of the day
Rose from the rustling woods and mounted high.
The talk of monkeys, and a whistling bird,
The tireless tolling of the barbet's bell,
The singing of the insects that I heard,
Had no strange tale to tell.

Then far away I heard a sambhur stag
Blurt sudden challenge in the plain beneath,
And at his signal 'twas as though a flag
Warned the whole forest of the walking death.
For, stealing through the woods came silent fear,
Its path betrayed before its footsteps passed;
And soon the belling of the spotted-deer
Told that it travelled fast.

The lower regions of the list'ning hill
Next gave their signal of that moving dread,
The squirrel's indignation ringing shrill,
Thrilling his warning through the woods ahead,
Hanging head downward in his frantic wrath,
With throat pulsating, while a chain of sound,
In high-pitched clinking, link by link sped forth,
The squirrel cursed the ground.

Still, of the thing itself that came so fast
I heard no single sound of voice or tread;
Only each signal station, as it passed,
An urgent message through the forest sped.
And next the monkeys, close below my stone,
Hooted in fury, dashing to and fro,
And in the frightened forest I alone
Knew not what passed below.

On soundless pad there passed that silent fear,
Around the wooded contour of the hill,
While in a glade below piped loud and clear
A plover's cry denouncing it as ill.
Down in the woods a nervous muntjak barked;
A crane rose squawking from a hidden pond;
And floating far I heard new sounds that marked
Fear in the plain beyond.

- John Still, *Poems in Captivity*, 1919.

Kalametiya
Kandy

Yala

Horton Plains

There is fear everywhere - in the silence and in the shrill calls and the wild cries, in the stirring of leaves and grating of branches, in the gloom, in the startled, slinking, peering beasts.

- Leonard Woolf,
The Village in the Jungle, 1913

Yala

Yala

Yala

Kalametiya

Horton Plains

It was in a wet valley that I saw one night a very beautiful sight of the kind that gives rise to superstitious fear. It was too high above sea-level for there to be any termites, being actually a part of Adam's Peak itself, so the fallen twigs and branches lay where they fell until agents slower than white ants ultimately consumed them. The night that I slept there was very dark, and it poured with rain, but the whole floor of the forest was lit by the phosphorescence of some fungus that had invaded the dead branches. Each was a silvery green bar of shimmering light, and our faces shone as the faces of the dead.

- John Still, *The Jungle Tide*, 1930

IV. Once upon a time the stones sang

Kelaniya

Of the Buddha and his message

Gautama Buddha, who taught the truth in such pleasant surroundings as the Deer Park and the Bamboo Grove, was born as Prince Siddhartha in the Lumbini garden near the city of Kapilavastu, on a Vesak full-moon day, more than two thousand five hundred years ago. The prince spent his childhood in the palace of his father, King Suddhodana, attended by pleasures suitable to his age. As a youth of wondrous beauty, he married Yasodhara, a virtuous maiden endowed with good looks, modesty and gentle bearing. Fearing that the prince may go to a penance grove, true to the words of the sage Asita, who predicted his goal as that of supreme enlightenment, the king saw to it that the young couple spent their time in pavilions suited to each season, surrounded by luxuries pleasing to the senses. A son, Rahula, was born in due course, and the king was delighted, thinking that paternal affection would strengthen the prince's bond to the royal family. But this was not to be.

The prince, who felt that life in the palace was like that in a prison, heard about the charm of the city groves and wished to visit them. He mounted a golden chariot drawn by horses of the best breed and went along the royal road, gazed at by citizens, their eyes wide open in excitement. Among these citizens, there was a feeble, old man with white hair, his hands resting on a staff, eyes veiled by the brows, and limbs hanging loose and bent. On hearing from the charioteer that old age comes upon all, the prince returned to the palace, perturbed. On a second occasion, he saw a man afflicted by disease, with his belly bloated, limbs emaciated and pale, panting, leaning on another for support. The sight that disturbed the prince on a third occasion was that of a corpse carried by four men, followed by others bewailing him. As he set out of the city on the fourth occasion, the prince met a mendicant who had relinquished the lay-life, for the sake of salvation, and he, too, decided to renounce the world, which he did at the age of twenty-nine. After six years of striving, under teachers and by himself, the bodhisattva Siddhartha arrived at the village of Uruvela in Gaya, where he overcame the forces of Mara, the Evil One, who tried to dissuade him, from his search for Truth. After a refreshing bath in the cool waters of the river Neranjara, the bodhisattva partook of the meal of milk-rice offered by the village-maiden Sujata, and went to a quiet spot nearby, where he sat cross-legged at the foot of a tree. And then, after hours of meditation, the Truth dawned upon him. He became an Enlightened One, earning the title Buddha for himself and the name Bodhi for the tree he sat under.

The Buddha taught the Truth he realised, viz. the unsatisfactory nature of life, the cause for this and the means of eradicating it. This he did by example and precept, until he passed away at the age of eighty. The many discourses that he delivered unfolded a way of life for all men and women, lay or ordained. The path he proclaimed has as its basic principles the avoidance of the extremes of indulgence and mortification; refraining from clinging to life, by destroying its root-cause, the thirst for worldly pleasures; abstaining from all evil arising out of greed, anger and ignorance; practising such noble virtues as loving kindness, compassion, benevolence and equanimity; and above all, restraining the mind, which leads to the goal of emancipation.

The bringing of the Buddha's message to Sri Lanka in the third century before the Christian era is the most momentous event in the island's history. The arahant Mahinda, son of emperor Asoka, was responsible for this deed of merit. The thera Mahinda arrived, journeying through the air (so the chronicles say), accompanied by four Elders, a novice and a lay disciple and alighted on the pleasant Missaka mountain that lay to the east of the city of Anuradhapura, on the full-moon day of the month of Poson. King Devanampiyatissa, ruler of Sri Lanka at the time, who had set forth to enjoy the pleasures of the chase, also came to mount Missaka, in pursuit of a stag, who was in fact a 'deva' in disguise. Addressing the king by the name Tissa, the thera said, "We are disciples of the King of Truth, O great king, come hither from compassion toward thee." This news was not altogether strange to Devanampiyatissa, for, in the course of an exchange of gifts, his friend, the monarch Asoka, had sent him a message saying, "I have taken refuge in the Buddha, his Doctrine and his Order. Seek then even thou refuge in these best of gems." Conversion was therefore quick and easy. The thera Mahinda preached the doctrine. The king and his followers became lay disciples. So did Queen Anula and her retinue in due course. Buddha's message spread among the people of the land under the patronage of the king. Monasteries were built for the monks to reside in, the first such being the Mahavihara in the Mahamegha garden, a pleasant park with an abundance of water and shade. More dwellings, refectories, bathing-tanks and buildings for repose were set up, as the community of monks grew in number. Thupas were built to enshrine the Buddha's relics that were brought from Jambudipa. The Order of nuns was established with the arrival of Sanghamitta and other nuns, who also brought a branch of the sacred Bodhi tree, which was planted in the Mahamegha grove.

Buddhism flourished under Devanampiyatissa and his successors, the most notable among them being Dutugemunu, who became king, succeeding Elara, a protector of tradition, though not one who knew the virtues of the three gems. Ruvanveliseya, Mirisaveti caitya and the Lohapasada are three of the many monuments set up during Dutugemunu's reign, to consecrate which elaborate ceremonies were held and lavish gifts of alms given. The picture we have of that age is one of virtuous monks and nuns residing in monasteries and teaching the Truth to pious lay-followers who attended to their needs, and let the doctrine they learned influence their way of life. Structures of wood and brick of those times have perished but some stone images and monuments remain, to proclaim the splendour that was. No less eloquent are facets of the Buddhist way of thinking that have left a lasting impact on the culture of the land.

- **Ratna Handurukande** (1996)

Mudunagala

Mihintale

Mihintale is covered with cells hidden in every nook and corner and perched upon the edge of precipices. They tell of an age even older than the coming of Buddhism when ascetics sought this hill as a refuge from the world. In the earliest days of Buddhism men lived in such jungle caves and meditated on the transience of all things on earth. From them it is said, Buddhist architecture gradually evolved. The caves began to be walled in with brick and plaster and entered by narrow doorways with stone door posts and lintels. They were enlarged inside and turned into rock temples, from which in course of time came the magnificent monasteries built of stone which are seen today.

- W. T. Keble, *Ceylon Beaten Track*, 1940.

Bellanwila

Anuradhapura

Our first introduction to Anuradhapura was in the early uncertain gleams of dawn, and passing glimpses of great castellated masses towering far above the prevailing forest imparted an air of romance and mystery which made us feel as if we were entering a veritable fairy-land. "More light" did not diminish the mystery nor yet dissipate the romance. The park-like domains surrounding the little town, the lakes, the forest drives, the palace pillars, all made up a first impression that stirred the imagination in favour of the supernatural.

- John Ferguson,
Ceylon in 1893.

Anuradhapura

Anuradhapura

Where once the clamour of great things
Filled all the thronging city ways
Now silence broods. no echo rings
Of all the grandeur of those days.

Where splendour once amazed the eye
With all the treasures of the east,
Now only woods and ruins lie
For wild things, bird and wandering beast.

But only ancient sanctity
Can linger in this large wild waste,
Where once the wealth of land and sea
Was built in lofty forms of earth.

A vast and joyous praise to be
For him who taught how all things haste
To death, because eternally
All life is hollow, even death.

This is a land of memories,
This place of sombre woods and ways
Tall trees and tranquil lakes. The days
Are full of magic secrecies.

Mysterious all things, hushed and deep
Oblivioned things that dream in vain
Thrilled ever in the kiss of sleep
Away from sunbeams and the rain.

- George Keyt, *The Buddhist*, Feb. 1940

The protection of the Bodhi Tree was ensured by guarding it from both humans and animals. The sprinkling of *paritta* water is a means of protecting it from the evil. Performing *Santi karma* (benedictory rites) by ritual priests is another method. There was also a third group that supplied the necessary objects needed to achieve the above two objectives. This group consisted of people like the smiths who supplied axes scissors and hoes, gold and silversmiths who made gold and silver pots, goblets, mirrors and lamps necessary for the ritual of offering alms and lighting. The curators of gardens grew flowers, and flower suppliers, the painters, the weavers, the cooks and tailors all performed their assigned functions. So we see that the institution created to maintain the sacred Bodhi Tree had a very large number of participants. It involved a large amount of human labour. When the *Sinhala Bodhivamsaya* speaks of *Bo-mangula* or the festival of the Bodhi Tree it is quite clear that there was such a ceremony in honour of the tree celebrated every year.

— H. S. S. Nissanka, *Mahabodhi Tree in Anuradhapura, Sri Lanka*, 1994.

Sacred Bo-Tree - Anuradhapura

Fifteen centuries ago Anuradhapura was a city of over three million people, a city of flowers and incense. The descriptions of it in the Mahawansa, including measurements of individual buildings and streets, are verified by every excavation so far made. Statements about Anuradhapura can be based on known facts rather than on deduction; and unusual, if not unique, circumstance in archaeological discovery. Here, without question, was a city ranking in importance with Ninevah and Babylon. The grandeur of its plan and buildings can be imagined after considering what remains of them. Studies show that with the quantity of bricks used to build the Ruanweli Dagoba alone, a wall a foot thick and ten feet high could be built from London to Edinburgh. The original height of Abayagiriya Dagoba was four hundred and fifty feet - the Washington Monument is only five hundred and fifty five - and the diameter of its dome was three hundred and sixty.

- Vinton Liddell Pickens, *Serendipity*, 1964.

Abeygiriya - Anuradhapura

Thuparama - Anuradhapura

If you sit on a ruined balustrade in the Thuparama Park at Anuradhapura, or upon a fallen pillar in the sacred quadrangle at Polonnaruwa, you cannot but feel moved to reflection that the monuments around you have a message, inasmuch as the lithic inscription we saw told its story more directly.

Yes, the ruins of our ancient cities have a message for us all, if we put ourselves in their surroundings. You can spend hours in such reflections. You may spend days in admiration and wonder. You may take years to study the styles and designs of the structure, and their relation to India, Persia and Egypt. You may do all this and eventually be able to track through the ages something Mycenaean, something Egyptian, something Sumerian, Aryan, Dravidian or early Brahmin - but yet fail to read aright the message of these stones, unless you seek and mentally grasp the conditions of their construction.

Disregard kingly power and monkish influence, wealth, the condition of labour and other such materialistic matters. Consider only the indispensable factors for the production of such excellence in craftsmanship. These are firstly, the existence of many skilled craftsmen – loving their art, and longing for the means of expressing their art, and, secondly, the co-existence of a public able to appreciate and ready to recognize the merits of good work. The two factors act reciprocally on each other, and the absence of either one injuriously affects the other.

But even this is insufficient. You must be responsive to the influence of these remains of the past, identifying and rendering yourself sensitive to their surroundings, and the manner of men who built these.

- Andreas Nell, in R. L. Brohier, *Discovering Ceylon*, 1973.

Having divided the width across the dagaba into five parts, (out of them) three parts are the height (of the dome). Bell-shape, Chatty-shape, Bubble-shape, Heap-of Paddy, Lotus-shape, and Nelli are the six kinds (of dagabas).
Having divided the width across the dagaba into five parts, the length (of the dagaba) is subdivided into twenty-four parts. For the three stories (or necklaces), take five and a half; the chamber (dome) eight; the four-sided enclosure of the Celestials *(devatas)* a couple and a half; the (other member of the enclosed) pair (one and a half); the last six for the spire; a half more for the *chatta*.

- Henry Parker, *Ancient Ceylon*, 1909.

Anuradhapura

The fair tree of thought that knows
no duality,
Spreads through the triple world.
It bears the flower and fruit of
compassion,
And its name is service of others.

Saraha's Treasury of Songs,
No. 188, 9th century, v 107.

In the Moon of Vesak

In the moon of Vesak quiet vehicles of memory
The Birth of Kindness in commemoration
The calm lantern like moons
the quiet breeze
Illumined whispers of a world in homage.

- George Keyt,
Ceylon Observer Annual, 1938.

Anuradhapura

Gal Vihara 1934 : A Recollection

(For my late and very dear friend Lionel Wendt)

It was felt that this production would have been incomplete without a contribution from Mr. Basil Wright, the famous film producer, who was responsible for that gem which he named "Song of Ceylon". Many consider this film, which was shot some 32 years ago, as the one that has best projected the image of the country, the soul of its people, and the endless beauty of its landscape with a subtle touch of magic for the world to see and admire.
Mr. Wright, in accepting the invitation to contribute an article, made no apology for not writing about tea and added, "If I have not written about tea this does not mean that I do not appreciate either the beverage or its history. It means, rather, that more than anything, I appreciate the beautiful country which gives it birth".

There are certain small patches of the earth's surface which have a character and influence so powerful that anyone who stands within their bounds is deeply and intimately affected. One of these – for me at least – is the Gal Vihare.
Up from the wiry grey-green grass in a treeless precinct juts, like a whale, an enormous outcrop of granite. From this living rock was carved, centuries ago and on a cyclopean scale, a fourfold image of the Buddha. As you face the rock, you see at its left end Buddha seated. His legs are crossed under him, and his hands rest palm-upwards on his lap. His head is held high; with sightless eyes he regards infinity. Move your eyes a little to the right, and there is a cave-shrine within which sits a smaller image of Buddha, canopied with stone flowers and a cobra's swelling hood. Next to this towers a standing figure, thought by some to represent the disciple Ananda weeping for his master, but more probably another image of Buddha. Fully thirty feet high, this great figure stands with hands folded across the breast, below which the draperies hang in

Gal Vihara - Polonnaruwa

stiff perpendicular folds.
Whether it is the effect of centuries of wind and rain, or whether the markings of the granite were originally so, or whether the sculptor took special advantage of the pattern of the stone, I cannot decide. Whatever the reason, the face has an expression of eternal sadness, eternal longing, eternal wonder.
To the right again, and finally, is the Buddha recumbent-a statue on an even larger scale. It is about fifty feet long; and as you stand before it the head of Buddha, resting on his bent arm as on a pillow, towers above you. His eyes are closed, his mouth pursed like a great rosebud, and in all that rounded face is to be seen the image of peace forever, the Nirvana which he alone attained.
His left arm lies quietly along the line of his side, following the pronounced contour of his hip. The folds of his robe, which reach as far as his feet, are disposed in horizontal placidity. On the soles of the feet are carved identical representations of the lotus flower.
If you go nearer to the Gal Vihare and step on to the burning floor of granite in front of the statues, you will see, as often as not, a little round basket containing rice and frangipanni. Perhaps it is a pingo-carrier who has been here with his two flat baskets swaying from his shoulder-yoke like a pair of scales. He puts down his burden, unlooses his headwrapping, loosens the folds of his sarong, and lays on Buddha's reclining elbow his humble offering. Then, after bending thrice in prayer, he walks backwards from the sleeping god, hitches up his skirt again, winds the simple white cloth round his head, picks up his load again and, with that swinging and rhythmic walk of a yoke-carrier, departs.
And when he is gone the sense of scale goes too. With no human figure for comparison, the great carvings are no longer great. They have no need to be enormous, no need to be tiny; they are beyond comparison, beyond consideration, belonging only to the nothingness of absolute peace. Yet is there not more than nothingness here? Rather must we see the Gal Vihare as a physical representation in stone of the great attributes of all godheads – meditation and understanding, sorrow-in-joy or joy-in-sorrow. The pebble cast into the still pool sends out a succession of concentric ripples; but within a few moments for us, a few centuries perhaps for a water-fly, all is again still.
So for me, one morning alone at the Gal Vihare, the backward and forward ripples of my restless western mind gradually came to rest, and I found peace.

- Basil Wright, *in: 100 years of Ceylon Tea*, 1967

Kaludiya Pokuna - Mihintale

Fringed by umbraceous trees, which dip their boughs in its placid depths, and with the hill offer inviting shade, the sheltered tarn has acquired for all time the pertinent designation Kalu-diya Pokuna, the 'Black-water pool'. Around the image of this winsome lake was laid out, with skilful adaptation to the varied levels and interspaces between the foot-boulders of the guardian hills, a complete monastery - isolated 'so near and yet so far' - from the gregarious Buddhistic establishments of Mihintale.

- J. M. Seneveratne, *Guide to Mihintale*, 1952.

Gal Vihara - Polonnaruwa

Gal Vihara - Polonnaruwa

I have kept to the last the best thing of all – indeed, to my mind, one of the best things in the whole world, of which I have seen a good deal. In the cool of the evening, walk or drive the short distance to the Gal-Vihare. It stands at the end of a glade. The little shrine is hewn out of the long low mass of living rock, with the huge Buddha sleeping, and the sleepless figure of his disciple Ananda watching, erect at his head . . . It is peace eternal – the most moving, yet most comforting sight in the East that I know. Never has death been so beautifully depicted...no Terrors here, only rest, infinite, deep, and abiding. In spirit, I often go back to that lovely little glade, at sunset, the hour of many cooing doves. I would say, (varying an ancient saying) :-

If there is a place of Peace upon Earth,
It is here, it is here, it is here.

- C. Brooke Elliot, *The Real Ceylon*, 1938

The Gal Vihara

The centuries assaulted it
With scourge of sun and flail of rain,
Waste of war and jungle sabotage
And the knowledge each enjoys for slow destruction.
Into the darkness of rank entanglement
The sanctum withdrew,
Veneration fell to sleep devotion came to end.
The scarred reliefs stood veiled
Immune from the witherings of weather,
The walls resolved to ruins only to expose
A mastery of achievement in a sacred grove,
A triumph of destination on a granite wall,

Now it is open to the light for all to see
Faith and apotheosis poised in a past creation;
To feel our fetters fall and evanesce before
A language in stone of endless tranquility;
To understand how deep down
The ancient craftsmen drove their years
With chisel and unfaltering knowingness
Into the hewn figures of their refuge
To breathe an air so rich in rest,
So abounding in intimate belief,
We hear silence for the first time
And waters flowing over the dry
River bed of our existence.

- W. R. McAlpine,
Death of the Beloved and other poems, 1991

Gal Vihara - Polonnaruwa

Looking at these figures I was suddenly, almost forcibly jerked clean out of the habitual, half-tied vision of things, and an inner clearness, clarity, as if exploding from the rocks themselves, became evident and obvious. The queer evidence of the reclining figure, the smile, the sad smile of Ananda standing with arms folded. The thing about all this is that there is no puzzle, no problem, and really no 'mystery.' All problems are resolved and every thing is clear, simply because what matters is clear. The rock all matter, all life, is charged with dharmakaya---everything is emptiness and everything is compassion. I don't know when in my life I have ever had such a sense of beauty and spiritual validity running together in one aesthetic illumination.

- Thomas Merton, *Asian Journal*, 1968

Lankatillake - Polonnaruwa

...a charming image house of five storeys for which – as it was adorned with ornaments of flowers and creepers and with figures of gods and Brahmas and embellished with buildings, with turrets, grottoes, apartments and halls – the name of Lankatilaka was befitting. In this (temple) he had erected a standing image which was an elixir for the eyes, which had the size of the living Buddha, which (likewise) was called Lankatilaka.

- *Culavamsa* II, 1953, 78,52-55.

Vatadage - Polonnaruwa

The growing Towers like Exhalations rise,
And the huge Columns heave into the Skies.

- Alexander Pope,
The Temple of Fame, 1712.

The wilderness is indeed highly interesting, not merely on account of its magnificent sylvan scenery, but also because there are many surprising heaps of ruins of great edifices scattered over its surface; all that a race now long extinct, or removed to other lands, have left behind them to indicate that here of old a potentate reigned and probably tyrannized over his subjects; that here fields were once cultivated and cities built by an industrious people; and that here the arts and sciences at least to a certain extent, had flourished.

- James Campbell, *Excursions, adventures and field-sports in Ceylon,* 1843.

Medirigiriya

In a lonely place, among leafless branches,
There are images seated in a circle,
There are placid faces and unseeing eyes
In everlasting silence
There are words spoken with voices from some-
where else,
Very soft, very distant
The words are spoken, uttered in vibration,
Around that lonely place,
And the desolation listens.

- George Keyt, *Poems*, 1936

Vatadage - Polonnaruwa

Vatadage - Polonnaruwa

In the northern part of the province of Rohana lies the district of Dighavapi. A cetiya and a monastery were built there by Saddhatissa who during the reign of his elder brother Dutthagamani, was in that district for many years busily engaged in the promotion of agriculture. The cetiya was considered to be a sacred one as there prevailed the belief that the spot on which the cetiya stood was visited by the Buddha. How a samanera who was engaged in white washing the cetiya slipped down but was miraculously saved from death is described in the Saratthappakasini. Dighavapi is also mentioned as another place where Maliyadeva preached the Chachakka Sutta. On one occasion it was announced that a Mahajatakabhanaka there would preach at Dighavapi the Mahavessantara Jataka, and we are told that a samanera went there from Tissamaharama covering on foot the long distance of nine yojanas.

- E.W. Adikaram
Early History of Buddhism in Ceylon, 1946
2nd imp-1953.

Digavapi

Wasgamuwa

Maduragala

The higher human being, the Buddha and the Arahats live
Like the lotus that is born of water
And yet untouched by the water.
- Gunadasa Amarasekera

Tantrimalai

On a one-inch map, twenty miles north-east of Anuradhapura is a dot. "Caves, ruins", says the writing beside it. This is Tantrimalai . . .

Imagine the amphitheatres of ancient Rome "blown up" many, many times. Imagine one of them with one half of its seating removed. Imagine the rest as a square mile of upheaved,undulating, grey-black rock, a series of frozen waves of stone, as John Still would have it, with a tiny tank for an arena. Grandeur made infinitely more awesome for its being in the middle of the wilderness. This is Tantrimalai.

A sedentary Buddha, colossal in stature, carved in the rock in high relief, the panels on either side of it prepared centuries ago but yet uncut centuries later : a reclining Buddha of giant proportions, the finishing touches yet to be made : a stock of wedged pillars and coping stones, beaded edges cut with great care, all lying in the forest where they were quarried; a stupa crumbling with age on the crest of the highest wave of stone, and leading to it a flight of steps that begins but does not end; a stone cubicle atop another pinnacle, a sentinel watching over the panorama; ruins everywhere, caves and inscriptions here and there. This Tantrimalai.

This is Tantrimalai, where carvings that rival Gal Vihare's await the sculptor's finishing strokes; where eight of a flight of steps are cut while a ninth remains half cut, edges as sharp as on that day the chisel was wielded; where pillars and stones, carved and uncarved, lie where they were quarried, awaiting buildings to be erected. This is Tantrimalai, as it was on that day when the word came that an army from the coast was on the march, the day when a people fled leaving their task unfinished. Only Time and Nature have wrought their ravages as the crumbled buildings attest.

- Subbiah Muthiah, *"The Unfinished City"*, *Times of Ceylon Annual*, 1959.

Medirigiriya

In the general cultural expansion throughout South East Asia by Hindu India, Sri Lanka was the first to be colonized and civilised. It was also the first country to receive from the India of emperor Asoka, the benisons of Buddhism in the reign of Devanampiya Tissa in the 3rd century B.C. Since that time Buddhist art and culture thrived and flourished to such an extent of grandeur and majesty that we look in amazement today at the strident gaudiness and sheer vulgarity of modern Buddhist art, if art it can be called, seen in too many of the temples and monasteries scattered about in the land, looking more like ostentatious erections influenced by florid injections of baroque and rococo architecture, and less like the austere and classically simple structures they should be.

It would appear that the great Buddhist sculptures of former times have virtually ceased to inspire us. They are never actually seen but always only casually noticed and taken for granted in the pious pilgrimages and *pujas* of the worshipper and if at all, just regarded as an encouragement to devotion. As against this in countries like Thailand, Japan and Nepal, it has been the reverse, where to this day there is aesthetic pleasure and also inspired veneration in the contemplation of both traditional and modern Buddhist art. But the essence of Buddhist sculpture has the power to stimulate in us an appreciation of the beauty that so enriches our cultural heritage. Memorable photographic artistry is an impressive vehicle of such communication.

- George Keyt (1901 - 1993).

A note written in 1989 on seeing Nihal Fernando's photographs of Buddhist art.

Maligavila

Maligavila

Maligavila

There are some wonderful remains at a place called Maligavela about 5 miles South East of Okkampitiya, three miles east of the Kumbukkan Oya, and ten miles south of the road from Wellawaya to Tuppane. It must have been a celebrated place at one time.

The remains are in the heart of a very fine forest. There is a profusion of stone pillars, and walled enclosures; some walls as much as 4 1/2 feet high standing intact with a fine smooth surface, the stones fitting together to a nicety. All sorts of objects are lying about; the place must have been very extensive.

Specially noteworthy is a colossal figure of Buddha now on its back and the head broken off but lying in its place. The length of this image from neck to bottom of robe is 31 feet and 11 feet across on a single stone; no rock near it, the head evidently was part of the same piece.

The figure stood on a pedestal (close to which it lies) which is 15 feet across at top, the stone is circular and all one piece, part broken away and a crack extending to centre aperture, the stone is hollow underneath and has evidently been explored for treasure.

- G. A. Baumgartner,
Government Agent, Uva Province
in a letter of 10 July 1897. Reproduced by
H. C. P. Bell, *C.A.L.R.* 1, 4, April 1916.

Piduragala

The caves at Piduragala are associated with the brief history of Sigiriya. The Piduragala rock is situated about a mile north of Sigiriya. Archaeological evidence indicates that they had been used by Buddhist anchorites in pre-Christian times. Close to the summit of the rock is a large cave in which reposed a colossal image of the recumbent Buddha, made of brick and stucco. One of the caves now serves as a vihara. Under its drip ledge is a record in Brahmi script.

- *Handbook for the Ceylon Traveller*, A Studio Times Publication, 2nd ed. 1983

Despite the acrid stench of bat droppings which frequently reaches the room from further back among the crevices, it is the *gal len*, stone caves, which are particularly prized by the monks. The special significance of these may be read from a small lip, or drip-ledge (*kataram*), cut along the front edge of the rock above the room. The practical purpose of the lip is to keep rain water from running back into the cave, which is therefore rendered habitable. To the monks, however, the drip-ledges embody the great antiquity, and therefore the great value, of the forest-dwelling life; ...In their view, just as laymen in the first days of Buddhism in Ceylon prepared caves for the monks, laymen refurbish the same caves today. As in ancient days, the laymen gain merit for their spiritual well-being, and the monk is set on the path to Nirvana.

In contemplating the drip-ledges, therefore, modern monks affirm their solidarity with their ancient forebears, and their writings are full of references to ancient rules, legends, and places. The first proposition is simply that the monks do indeed follow in detail an ancient way of life.

- Michael Carrithers,
The Forest Monks of Sri Lanka, 1983

Magulmaha Vihara - Yala

At whatever period of a man's life, the urge in him for the ascetic life asserts itself, then along with the other bonds binding to the worldly life, the bonds of blood-relationship also lose their force. The mother has become an elder sister; the father has become a brother; the wife has become a sister; the son has become a brother... fellow beings, fellow sufferers.

- Sumana Samanera,
A Call to Buddhist Monkhood, 1961.

Bundala

Ritigala

Ritigala - A Monastic Mountain

(for Joan Budgen)

Discharged from the brutal belly of Earth
When havoc hurled nature apart at birth
By might of fierce galactic hammerblows,
The walking world struggling in embryos
Of monstrous proportions of fire and rock,
Air and fever-heat of seas, to unfrock
The nightmare of disorder and ordain
An ordered end to the raging terrain,
It rises sheer aloof in solitude,
Asleep in battle's aftermath subdued.

The first rays fell upon its head
Cloud aureoles gathered and led
Rain-vapour to the desert dawn
Of its dead nakedness to spawn
A cell to fracture into life,
And urge the nub of root to strife
In its journey upwards to sight,
To spread and clothe in green of light
Its rawness, and from soil exhale
A jungle tortured from travail.

From plains came early man,
Harsh, grotesque, simian,
Brains attuned to rhythms
Of darkfull and brutal hymns
To blood-gods' appeasements
In the Fanh's elements.
Caves, boulder-bound on spurs,
Fear's haunted harbingers,
Housed their ferocity.
And stone identity.

- W. R. McAlpine,
Death of the Beloved and other poems, 1991

Ritigala

The principal common feature of the *padhanaghara pirivenas* or forest monasteries of the *pansukulikas* is the double-platform building: raised platforms formed by retaining walls of massive stone, found in pairs, linked together by a stone bridge. The main axis of the combined platforms is invariably set east-west. The eastern platform is usually rectangular in plan and, judging by the absence of column bases, appears to have been open and without a superstructure. The eastern platform is usually square and smaller than its companion. The existence of column bases in four rows of four suggests a superstructure supporting a roof with the building, divided into eight or nine separate rooms. The open platform can be reached by stone steps in the centre of the eastern retaining wall, while access to the bridge is by either of the two stone flights running between the platforms.

- W.R. McAlpine and David Robson
A Guide to Ritigala, 1983.

Bana

Name and form cannot save you he said
There is no path through the sky
You are pitted against the absolutes
Of madness, death and decay
The world is the foam of illusion
There is only the pilgrims way
Which winds inward ever and ever
Into the question : Who am I?

- Jane Russell,
Ganga - Poems (1974 - 78)

In most lands archaeology deals with temples whose last worshipper died long centuries ago. No one now prays to Horus or to Pallas Athene (not under that name); but here in the forests of Ceylon the ruins we explore are those of a religion still living, to this day the faith of the majority of the population.

- John Still,
The Jungle Tide, 1930

Batalagoda - Ibbagamuwa

Polonnaruwa

Though the treasure-seekers had removed all the objects deposited in this chamber as well, our labours were rewarded by an important discovery made therein. Its walls also were painted, and the paintings on two of its sides are in a satisfactory state of preservation. The paintings depict divine beings among clouds which have cut off the lower parts of their bodies. The figures have been sketched in outline only, red and black being the pigments used, but are of high artistic quality indicating that the artist possessed skill in draughtsmanship, a subtle sense of form and an understanding of the principles of balanced composition. Against a possible contention that what we see in the chamber are all that the artists intended to complete, and that the paintings are impressionistic sketches, is the presence of a vertical line dividing each scene into two-a line which must have been drawn by the artist as an aid to balanced grouping of the figures. Water had stagnated in this chamber for a considerable time after the treasure-seekers had left it open, and before it was filled in by the collapse of the sides of their digging. The plaster of the lower portion of the walls had decayed due to this; happily, however, there were no figures there. The presence of divine beings hovering about the upper reaches of Mount Meru is in accordance with the cosmological beliefs of the ancients.

In addition to their artistic worth, these paintings are of interest in that they show that the figures in the Sigiri paintings had been cut below the waist by the clouds of set purpose and not, as some try to maintain, due to the unevenness of the rock surface. They are also of value in understanding the purpose of the lines below the waist, (apart from certain lines in one figure, the genuineness of which are open to question) of the figures in the faint traces of paintings noticed in a cave (No. 7 in the plan published in Bell's Report for 1905) at Sigiri. The vagueness of these lines is full of such possibilities that they have been variously "copied" as bathing dresses, foundation garments and bifurcated garments. By comparing these faint traces with the better preserved paintings now brought to light, it is possible to come to a definite conclusion that what have been taken as bifurcated garments are the lines indicating peaked clouds in front of figures moving in heaven. The figures are cut above the knees horizontally by the clouds, and their conical peaks "bifurcate" the garment which drapes the body from the waist downwards.

- S. Paranavitane, *A.S.C.A.R.*, 1951

Mihintale

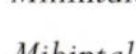

Mihintale

The key went into the lock and the door swung back showing a slit of blackness through which I passed into the cool darkness of the cavern temple. There could hardly be a more romantic setting than these caves with the dim light falling upon rows of motionless images and picking out the painted figures which crowd the roof and walls back to the remotest niches and corners: while in the deep silence of the vaulted sepulchre the water drips drop by drop from the ceiling into the great stone cistern on the floor of the cave.

- W. T. Keble, *Ceylon, Beaten Track*, 1940.

Mulkirigala

Degaldoruwa

Dambulla - Rock Temple

The temples which give this place celebrity, are parts of a vast cavern in the south side of the rock, at a height of about three hundred and fifty feet above the plain. The approaching to them is up the eastern shelving extremity of the rock, through an archway of masonry, and along a narrow platform of solid rock open to the south, enclosed by a low wall, shaded by trees, and containing in its area a cistern holding rain water, a very small temple and a bogah. This approach, platform and front raised our expectations very little, and did not at all prepare us for what we discovered on entering the temples. The wihare we explored is the last in order from the entrance. It is about fifty four feet long, and twenty seven wide; and its shelving roof, which dips gradually inwards, where most lofty, is about twenty seven feet high. The figures are well executed and brilliantly painted, and most of them are as large or larger than the ordinary size of man. The roof and sides of the rock and the front wall are painted of the brightest colors, and illuminated with a number of figures chiefly of Boodhoo. The general effect of the whole is striking and pretty.

- James Campbell, *Excursions, adventures and field-sports in Ceylon,* 1843.

"This mass of flowers, fresh-bred, fragrant and choice, I offer at the sacred lotus-feet of the Noble Sage. Even as these flowers must fade, so does my body march to a state of destruction."

- Buddhist Invocation.

Carved out of living rock, this almost free-standing statue at Aukana reaches high and beautiful 39 feet above its lotus decorated plinth. It is interesting to observe that this plinth has been carved separately and placed under the feet of the image.

As you walk towards this 1,500-year-old statue, you are at first struck not so much by its beauty but by the immensity of the task undertaken by the unknown sculptor. The mind quails at the thought of the many millions of steps taken by this genius as he walked, back and forth from the statue, working out its proportions which are perfect from whichever point it is viewed.

The best time of the day to view this statue is at dawn. The first rays of the morning sun bring out the rich hues of the rock image and makes it seem to come alive against the deep-green of the trees beyond. As the sun rises higher, it reveals the serenity of the exquisitely carved face: rising higher still,the sunlight picks out the gracefully carved robe, each pleat of which is a triumph of art. Looking at the statue, from atop the ruins opposite, one gets the impression that the image is being viewed through the wrong end of a telescope as it now appears much smaller than you expected it to be. Is it the perfect proportions, or the deliberate, yet subtle, distortion of the proportions of this rock-hewn creation that makes it look almost a miniature and a perfect one at that?

It is thought that this statue was sculpted during the reign of King Dhatusena, the great tank builder, who was to die tragically at the hands of his demented son, Kasyapa. The appalling story is often related of how Kasyapa, lusting for his father's fabled treasures, had the great patriarch imprisoned and tortured. The king, realising his end was at hand, promised to reveal the whereabouts of his 'secret treasure' if he was allowed to bathe in his beloved Kalavapi (today's Kalawewa) which he had built.

- *Handbook for the Ceylon Traveller*, 2nd ed., 1983.

Kelaniya

Polonnaruwa

Polonnaruwa

Epilogue

How should one value this great tradition, and how should one regard the ancient monuments of Ceylon? There must naturally be a difference in valuation as the beholder is different. To the Sinhalese Buddhist, it must mean something more than it could mean to anyone else. But there is nearly a millennium between the ancient tradition and the present. Besides, there is the rift which some five hundred years and more of foreign rule have made in ways of life and of thought. Just as the Indian settlers came to an island in which primitive cults were replaced by Buddhism, so it might seem that the West came to Ceylon in the sixteenth century, and has since then been responsible for a 'spiritual' and material conquest of the island. But in both these cases what truly belonged to it was never lost, it persisted, ready to issue forth again. Recent events show how strongly it has flowed underground, and how intensely it can gush out.

Whether in the altered social and economic structure of Ceylon, where 'all's changed now', these waters can be a healing source or a bitter potion, only the collective wisdom of all the present-day inhabitants of Lanka, and not of the Sinhalese alone, must decide. But this would be the subject of another study.

Whatever the future may bring, to all those who come to the ancient monuments of Ceylon, they must possess a value and a character. They may chasten our pride, amaze our intellects, or move our feelings, but it is well to remember that even their computations are values of limited currency. The sensibilities of the majority of men are so hardened today that if any one single priceless possession of the world's art were to disappear, it would apparently make little difference to the sum of things. The scale of what we are now asked to comprehend is so vast, that it would be prudent to be unmoved if Chartres were to be destroyed, and a bomb obliterated Athens. It may be that only little of the ancient art of Ceylon could be placed beside the wealth of ancient Egypt, or Rome or India; but such things as the *vahalkada* at Mihintale, the moonstones at Anuradhapura, the statue of the king at Polonnaruva, and Sigiriya, stand in their own right of excellence as records of artistic achievement, in no need of support from comparative judgement or prejudice.

The aesthetic emotion has been variously described in various cultures, but one might, in general, understand by it that state of feeling – of pleasure or joy – removed for the time being from practicality, and created by the contemplation of an artistic object which continues to stimulate our reactions. There is in the feeling created a species of growth which, as our senses return to the object, receives new impulses through our delighted attention to it. The Indian conception is thus put by Melle Auboyer in connection with the paintings of Ajanta: 'The aim of the painter... is to produce in the spectator a psychic state called sentiment (*rasa*) or more properly savour. This is the science of the hidden significance of external appearances, of the formation of a traditional mental image to be projected to the sensibility of the spectator, arousing in him a subjective sentiment... The painter...determines the form and produces artificially in the spectator certain sentiments equally artificial but also beneficial in kind.'[1]

Polonnaruwa

The ground common to these descriptions is an area of feeling which the transformation of reality produces in the sensitive spectator. No such spectator confronting the best of the art of the ancient tradition of Ceylon could fail to respond aesthetically. There is, in ancient Buddhist thought, an emotion described as a state of serene joy derived from the contemplation of a Buddha image – assuredly its strongest components may be religious, but in its essence this, too, is an aesthetic emotion. So whether one is a Buddhist or not, there could be aroused in one the emotion of *Buddhalambapiti* as one stands before the sedent Buddha at Anuradhapura, or sees the statues in the Gal Vihara at Polonnaruva.

- E. F. C. Ludowyk,
The Footprint of the Buddha, 1958.

1. Quoted by S. Paranavitane, *Art and Architecture of Ceylon*, 1954

V. A village folk tale

Ehetuwewa

HOMECOMING
My grandmother, silver-haired and frail,
sitting on a mat, with the betel tray next to her,
used to spin endless tales
in those monsoon evenings, when
dark ropes of dusk coiled in the air.
My brother and I were turned into
statues of clay, kneaded in her narratives.
She told us stories of kings and demons,
beasts and flowers; one evening, I remember
well,
a bird escaped from her story, rose to the sky,
flapped its wings, flew higher and higher, and
disappeared like a dot in the darkening sky.
Forty years later, the bird has come back,
wiser, if a little weaker, to roost in my mind.
It's a large bird with a long beak
and brown feathers. I'll show it to my kids
when they come back from school.

- Wimal Dissanayake,
Journal of South Asian Literature, (Michigan), 1987.

Ulhitiya

The houses are often built of timber and clay, and sometimes only of posts and leaves: they are rather smaller than English cottages, and never consist of more than one floor. The most common roof is formed of the leaves of the co-coa-nut tree. They are split lengthways through the middle of the centre nerve, and the fibres are plaited together, thus forming sheets of mat-ting about six feet in length and two feet broad. When disposed on the roof, one sheet laps over another; and this kind of thatch makes a house cooler, and excludes rain better than any other materials used within the tropics.

\- Rev. James Cordiner,
A Description of Ceylon, Vol. 1, 1807

Ehetuweva

The huts or dwellings are commonly situated in rather sheltered situations. They are usually constructed of mud, composed of a ferruginous earth; and in the maritime provinces, they are thatched with coconut leaves, in the Kandyan country with paddy straw. They are surrounded by a clump of trees, most commonly the jak-tree, coconut tree, and the plantain tree. The dwellings are built separate from one another: each hut being, in a certain degree, independent. The floors are of clay, and are occasionally covered with a dilute mixture of fresh cow-dung with water, which serves the purpose of keeping off insects. The villages are sometime surrounded by a deep ditch, as protection against elephants.

- Henry Marshall,
Ceylon, 1846

Ulhitiya

Galgiriya

Migahaweva

The open ground along the front of the house is clean, and free from grass and weeds, and is swept every morning. In this space, called the midula, there is a stand of peeled sticks supported on thin posts, and having a stick platform about four feet, or a little more, in length and two feet in width, raised three feet from the ground, with often another similar platform below it. On these are laid, after being washed, the blackened earthenware cooking pots of the house, and spoons made of segments of coconut shell with long wooden handles, which are used with them.

In the little kitchen at the end of the house, with a lean-to-roof, the hearths or fire-places called lipa are formed of three round stones fixed on the ground, about eight inches apart, on which are set the cooking pots, over a fire of dry sticks. Sometimes a separate small shed is built as a kitchen, but often the cooking is done inside the single apartment of the house, at one end of it. In each garden are a number of Coconut trees, some thin Halmilla trees, and often a Mango tree, or a dark-leaved Jak tree, with its enormous light green fruit hanging on pedicles from the trunk or larger branches, as well as a Lime tree, and four or five clumps of Plantain stems nearer the dwelling. Round the base of one or two of the Coconuts or Halmilla trees are piled on end long bundles of fire-wood, nearly two feet thick and six or eight feet long, the unconsumed sticks from the chena, collected by the women, tied round with creepers, and carried home on their heads. Climbing up a small tree in front of the house is a fine Betel vine, which is watered every day during the dry weather. We notice that a bleached skull of a bull is fixed among the leaves to guard the creeper from the unlucky glance of the "Evil Eye", which might cause its premature decay. In the damper ground adjoining the rice field a few slender Areka palms are growing, with their clusters of small fruit hanging below their leafy crowns.

- H. Parker,
Village Folk Tales of Ceylon, vol. 1, 1910.

The rains will come with the stinging thorn
And the ninth-month wave
Hurled to the heart.

Of the mud-house. Wet, dry, round
We shall be washed
With the morning.

And cockburst. Weep Mother into the lake
Into the pool, the sound, the flowers
The chaos of hours.

Bind us in the pool of tears
With the splendid rose
Of the morning . . .

– Meary James Tambimuttu,
Out of this War, 1941

Teldeniya

Hikkaduwa

off Galgamuwa

The peasant family lives in a room a little more (if at all) than 12 by 10 feet. It has a door - usually adzed and rarely of sawn timber, which affords egress from a frontal verandah 2 to 3 feet wide. The interior of the room is dark, for very rarely is a window provided. It sometimes found ventilation through a small opening set high up in the wall with wooden bars for protection. It merits remark in parenthesis, that a dwelling is oriented north or south, east or west, the reason for which I shall later explain, and that the door is slung to open inwards into the room - so that it can be readily shut and barred against forcible intrusion from outside.

A thatched leanto at the back of the dwelling serves as the kitchen. The fire-place or lipa, on which cooking is done, consists of three suitably selected stones on which the clay cooking vessel, called chattie, is placed after the fire is kindled under it. Two substantial meals are cooked each day, often co-operatively, by the women of the family.

- R. L. Brohier, *Discovering Ceylon*, 1973

Entrance to a village house -Galgamuwa

Embilipitiya

The threshing of the stacks is a business of great importance, which must be performed according to ancient customs that are supposed to have a magical effect, and prevent injurious demoniacal interference with the out-turn. After the floor has been thoroughly cleaned and purified, a magical circular diagram, with mystical symbols round it, is drawn on the ground round a central post, before the threshing can be commenced.

The unthreshed rice is laid over the floor in a circle round the central post, and four buffaloes in a row are driven over it, round and round the post, following the direction taken by the sun, that is, from the east towards the south and so on through the circle, the stems of the rice being shaken up from time to time. After the corn has been thus trampled out of the ears, it is collected and poured gradually out of baskets held high in the air, so that the wind may blow away the chaff. The corn is then placed in sacks and carried to the store.

- Henry Parker,
Village Folk Tales of Ceylon, 1910, Vol. 1

In Ancient Kotmale

In the beautiful principality, in Kotmale
I will build my house of the good soil's brick
With the timber of the ringing forests,
And I will cover it with the tiles flat,
One on one, as the palms of the farmers -

And in the morning will I see
The sun wounded as my heart with a million
arrows,
Rise between the mountain ranges
And spread in the green valley its golden blood.

And I will go into the fields in the seasons -
I will sow the grain, a stream between my hands,
I will cast the grain in falling nets,
And it will stream up round the calves of maidens
From the viridian fire of that clay.

And in the kilns of my sun-wed fields,
And under the haven of passing clouds
As I repose, in those almost everlasting days,
In the time ordained, in green calendars
Will come my yearned harvest.

- Lakdasa Wikkramasinha,
Poems, 1965 - 1970 (1973).

Kotmale

Kotmale

Tank Bund
Gal Oya

John Still's empathy for the island, and its culture was all-embracing. He was especially familiar with village life and custom, and, in his poem on an old woman who refused to leave her home even as the tide of jungle encroached upon her, this yearning to stay close to one's roots is, perhaps, most movingly expressed.

Blind Dingiri

Hide her in the thorny bine,
Poison berries overhead
Safe where living tendrils twine
Wreaths of scarlet for the dead.

Hide her where the vipers creep
Patterned by the chequered shade,
Lidless eyes that never sleep,
Watch for her the gods betrayed.

Lead her where the leopard cubs
Play as kittens lately born;
Guide her where the sambhur rubs
Velvet from his hardening horn.

- John Still,
The Jungle Tide, 1930.

Nildanda Hinna

Ehetuwewa

They level these Hills into narrow Allies, some three, some eight foot wide one beneath another, according to the steepness of the Hills, working and digging them into that fashion that they lye smooth and flat, like so many Stairs up the Hills one above another. The waters at the top of the Hills falling downwards are let into these Allies, and so successively by running out of one into another, water all; first the higher Lands and then the lower.

- Robert Knox, 1681

The calm beauty of these inland lakes is indescribable. The bright blue of the still water, the ring of white sand fringed with grass and forest, mingled greens and browns, the varied bird and animal life – and with all that wondrous hush which pervades and sanctifies nature uninvaded by man's encroachment -

'Oh! if there be an Elysium on earth,
It is this, it is this.'

- H. C. P. Bell, *A.S.C.A.R.*, 1896

Burst you wild-wood into fine rich blossom,
Caress the blooms, soft rain, fall unceasing
Let beauty also show on waists, willow, slim,
and lissome -
And my own girl, precious pearl, haunt my
dreaming.

- Sinhala love poem: tr. Patrick Fernando,
Ceylon Observer Pictorial, 1965

Lihiririyagama

Deniyaya

Udappu

... and Oriental conflagrations of costume! The walking groups of men, women, boys, girls, babies – each individual was a flame, each group a house afire for color. And such stunning colors, such intensely vivid colors, such rich and exquisite minglings and fusions of rainbows and lightnings! And all harmonious, all in perfect taste, never a discordant note: never a color on any person wearing at another color on him or failing to harmonize faultlessly with the colors of any group the wearer might join. The stuffs were silk - thin, soft, delicate, clinging; and, as a rule, each piece a solid color; a splendid green. a splendid blue, a splendid yellow, a splendid purple, a splendid ruby, deep and rich with smouldering fires - they swept continuously by in crowds and legions and multitudes, glowing, flashing, burning, radiant, and every five seconds came a burst of blinding red that made a body catch his breath and filled his heart with joy.

- Mark Twain,
Following the Equator, 1900.

Udappu

The Sinhala and Tamil New Year festivals are spent in the observance of age-old customs, folk dancing and national games like coconut shies, elephant races, hackery races, climbing the greasy pole and pillow-fighting. A common feature is the playing of the *rabana* (large bass drum with open bottom) by girls and women dressed in their best.

- *Handbook for the Ceylon Traveller*, 2nd ed. 1983.

Talduwa

Toddy tapped from the coconut flower is made into treacle or jaggery, a coarse brown candy. Vinegar is a by-product of toddy. From toddy is also distilled the national drink of the Island - Arrack. But toddy itself is an invigorating drink very popular along the south west coast.

The dried kernel of the coconut - copra - is finely grated and marketed as desiccated coconut which is used extensively in confectionery and cooking, mainly abroad. From copra is extracted coconut oil, used in the Island as a cooking fat and in the manufacture of soap, margarine and hair dressings, among other things. After the oil is extracted, the residue, poonac, is used as an animal food.

Along the south coast of the Island, cottagers leave the fibrous husk to soak in pits. Later, they are beaten to extract the fibre - coir. The coir is either spun into ropes or made into doormats, brooms, brushes and a number of other utility articles, which are now used the world over.

- *Handbook for the Ceylon Traveller,* 2nd ed. 1983.

Paiyagala
Negombo

Polonnaruwa

Medirigiriya

And beautiful as is much of Ceylon, and interesting as are its historical remains, the Sinhalese themselves are what makes the Island, for me and I hope for you an unforgettable and cherished memory.

- R. Raven-Hart,
Ceylon : History in Stone, 1964

Nuwara Eliya

Katnoruwa

Sinhalese countrymen are almost always handsome and often really lovely, with straight classical noses and cleanly - modelled lips; and both men and women have magnificent bodies and walk like happy gods.

- R. Raven Hart,
Ceylon : History in Stone, 1964

The Kandyan plough is only what may be called a crooked piece of wood, something like an elbow; it merely tears up the ground as unevenly as if it were done by hogs. They then overflow the field with water. They plough twice before they sow; but before they give the first ploughing, they let it water upon the land, in order to make it soft and the easier to be worked. After it is once ploughed, they usually make up the banks; for if they were to put off doing so till after the second ploughing, the soil would have become mere mud, totally unfit for banking. These banks are indispensable, not only as paths for the people to walk upon through the fields, who otherwise must go in the mud, but also to keep in and contain the water overflowing the ground.

- James Campbell,
Excursions, adventures and field-sports in Ceylon, 1843.

Wasgamuwa

Rekawa

The farmer is often described as fit to be a king, if the mud is washed off. Today, with or without mud, he has a sense of being left out of a cash based consumer society.

- Nihal Fernando, 1997.

Panahaduwa

Bellihul Oya

People in places

No races reflect their past history more faithfully than the peoples of Ceylon. Each of the races of the Island is clay of the pit whence it was dug, and each has been shaped and moulded by the long story of its past adventures: each has been burned in the fire of tribulation and come out with its characteristics burned deep into its members. The bright precocious spoilt child I had met upon the road, and his gentle timid sister carrying a water pot, were like a book of history in which a man might read the story of a wild adventure long ago; when a prince from India landed on an unknown Island; of a new faith that burned like a fire in men's hearts; of a great age of art and architecture and mighty kings; of a long desperate killing struggle for mastery over the invaders; of civil wars and three foreign conquests; of the decline of kings and the ascendency of chiefs; and of the rising of the morning star of a new awakening.

- W. T. Keble,
Ceylon Beaten Track, 1940.

Negombo

In the sun born over and over,
I ran my heedless ways.

- Dylan Thomas

Anuradhapura

Tripping gay and tripping light,
Your complexion pure and bright
As gold, your tresses shining black
Combed down your graceful back;
Arms so lithe and lovely, wound
Round pitcher's neck: are you bound
For the river thus, my lady,
Tripping carefree, lightly, gaily.

- Sinhala love poem: tr. by Patrick Fernando
Ceylon Observer Pictorial, 1965.

About once in a couple of years, a party of Gypsies who speak Telugu, and broken Tamil and Sinhalese, come along the high road, and settle down on a patch of open grass near a tank. The talipot palm leaves with which their diminutive oblong huts are roofed, and strong creepers or bamboos curved in a semicircle, for making the skeleton framework, are transported on small donkeys, the women and children carrying the other few household goods and cooking utensils in bundles on their heads. Some take about with them large numbers of goats.

As soon as they have raised their little huts, each about four feet high, and surrounded by a shallow channel for carrying off rain water, the adults leave them in charge of the children and old women, and spread through all the villages of the neighbourhood in order to collect food or money. The man carried in a round, flat, black basket slung in a cloth from his shoulder, a cobra or two, which are made to "dance", a term which means merely sitting coiled up (the head with the hood expanded being raised about fifteen inches from the ground) and making attempts to strike the moving knee or hand of the crouching exhibitor. The women tell fortunes by the lines on the hands.

All the village girls endeavour to raise the requisite three halfpence or twopence so as to hear, often for the third or fourth time, of their past and future experiences, and to be promised handsome husbands possessing fields and cattle. The adults pay a little rice for the exhibition of the cobras.

- H. Parker, *Village Folk Tales of Ceylon*, vol. 1, 1910.

Kurunegala

Kurunegala

Kurunegala

So doth the potter sitting at his work, and turning the wheel about with his feet, who is always carefully set at his work; and maketh all his work by number.
He fashioneth the clay with his arm, and boweth down his strength before his feet; he applieth himself to lead it over; and he is diligent to make clean the furnace.
All these trust to their hands: and every one is wise in his work.
Without these cannot a city be inhabited: and they shall not dwell where they will, nor go up and down.
They shall not be sought for in public counsel, nor sit high in the congregation: they shall not sit on the judge's seat, nor understand the sentence of judgement: they cannot declare justice and judgement, and they shall not be found where parables are spoken.
But they will maintain the state of the world, and all their desire is in the work of their craft.

— *Ecclesiasticus*, xxxviii

Tambuttegama
Tambuttegama

Arise and go down to the potters house, and there I will cause thee to hear my words. Then I went down to the potter's house, and behold, he wrought a work on the wheels.

- Jeremiah,
Ch. 18, 2-3

A lord who to a child like me
Would often say come hither
And ask of childish joys and griefs
Where could you find such another

He taught us alpha, beta . . . omega.
And sang the songs the letters sing.
He told us the tales the letters tell.
He fed us milk-rice, *kavun*, *kokis*, under the
brass lamp's silvery light.
And his gentle, caring hand steered our snail-
like feet 'toward the grove of Academe.'
Sinhala and Tamil without tears.
Didn't the poet say 'heaven lies about us in our
infancy'?

– Robert Silva, 1996

Panahaduwa

Sunetra Devi Rajamahavihara

There is something infectious in the sense of gaiety and atmosphere generated by village people, for their pleasures are very simple, as simple as their thoughts.

- R. L. Brohier,
Discovering Ceylon, 1973.

Colombo

Kirinde

Hambantota

Badulla

Hettipola

In the watch-hut by the field

Now withered are the things that were planted long ago;
The fences which were built then are broken by the bulls;
Protecting through the night the tender growth, the rice,
Drowsily let us sing the verses we devise.

Drop by drop the rain, which falls all over, gathers;
Rivulets and streams and cataracts, filling, will overflow;
Little by little lost will be the rice field getting covered;
Staying a little in places, I come to the hut to watch.

- tr. by George Keyt,
Poetry from the Sinhalese, 1938

Hikkaduwa

Negombo

Your children are not your children.
They are the sons and daughters of Life's
longing for itself.
They come through you but not from you,
And though they are with you yet they
belong not to you.
You may give them your love but not your
thoughts,
For they have their own thoughts.
You may house their bodies but not their souls,
For their souls dwell in the house of
tomorrow, which you cannot visit, not
even in your dreams.
You may strive to be like them, but seek not
to make them like you.
For life goes not backward nor tarries with
yesterday.
You are the bows from which your children
as living arrows are sent forth.

– Kahlil Gibran,
The Prophet

Mawanella

The Cinnamon Peeler

If I were a cinnamon peeler
I would ride your bed
and leave the yellow bark dust
on your pillow.

Your breasts and shoulders would reek
you could never walk through markets
without the profession of my fingers
floating over you. The blind would
stumble certain of whom they approached
though you might bathe
under rain gutters, monsoon.

Here on the upper thigh
at this smooth pasture
neighbour to your hair
or the crease
that cuts your back. This ankle.
You will be known among strangers
as the cinnamon peeler's wife.

I could hardly glance at you
before marriage
never touch you
– your keen nosed mother, your rough
brothers.
I buried my hands
in saffron, disguised them
over smoking tar,
helped the honey gatherers. . .

When we swam once
I touched you in water
and our bodies remained free,
you could hold me and be blind of smell.
You climbed the bank and said

this is how you touch other women
the grass cutter's wife, the lime burner's
daughter.

And you searched your arms
for the missing perfume

and knew

what good is it
to be the lime burner's daughter
left with no trace
as if not spoken to in the act of love
as if wounded without the pleasure of a scar.

You touched
your belly to my hands
in the dry air and said
I am the cinnamon
peeler's wife. Smell me.

- Michael Ondaatje,
The Cinnamon Peeler and other poems, 1992.

Ambalama

"Does the road wind uphill all the way?
Yes, to the very end.
Will the day's journey take the whole long day?
From morn to night, my friend.

But is there for the night a resting place?
A roof for when the slow, dark hours begin.
May not the darkness hide it from my face?
You cannot miss that inn."

Though taken out of their native context, these lines of Christina Rossetti are apt here. An ambalama in its primary sense meant a resting place for pilgrims on the road to - holy land. Only later did it come to mean also a trading post, a mart.

Its construction was of the simplest. A platform about a foot high and four stone blocks on it. Four logs on the four stone blocks forming a square or rectangle. Pillars rising from the logs, supporting a roof, thatched or tiled. Carved with masterful grace on the woodwork were motifs (geometrical, floral, animal) figures (dancers, musicians) and scenes (dancing, village feasts and processions).

Ambalamas were also places of fun and frolic, as folk rhymes and poetry testify. For instance–

The ambalama's Pina, Pina
Fetched a load of pots (gena, gena)
The ambalama's cart bull (gona, gona)
Smashed the whole darn'd lot
The peals and peals of laughter (hina, hina)
Seemed like they'd never stop

– Robert Silva, 1996

Ambalama

Panavita Ambalama

Panavita interior

Detail of granite column, Embekke

Embekke

See the girls that bathe in the pool
The heat that burns them to cool.
They put flowers in their hair
The scent of which brings the
Bees to such honey
And cads to suck toes . . . for a start
– Robert Silva, 1996.

Attaragollewa
Polonnaruwa

Folk Poems - dialogue

Why do you hold down your cloth, sister,
Why cover your breasts with your hand?
Why walk alone with no man beside you?
Shall we linger awhile in this ambalama?

I'm holding my cloth away from the mud,
My breasts are full of milk for my baby;
My husband's young brother isn't far behind
And night is falling, brother, farewell!
- Ashley Halpé, *Homing and other poems,* 1993.

From the 2nd century A.D. onwards reference to medical services appear frequently in the records. The physician king Buddhadasa (A.D. 341) provided dispensaries throughout the kingdom and ordained that there should be a resident hospital with a physician in charge for every ten villages: 'the first meting of this ancient grouping, *gandhaya*, which still survives in name in certain districts' (Codrington). He built 'halls along the roads' for the crippled and the blind. He also appointed veterinary surgeons to attend on cattle and elephants.

Wonderful operations are credited to this king, and he is said to have always carried his surgical instruments 'in his waist' and operated on the sick whom he met, including animals; and to have habitually visited in person the hospitals in his kingdom and discussed cases with the doctors. He is also credited with the authorship of a medical work, the *Saratha Sangraha*, written in Sanskrit, which is extant.

– H. Parker,
Ancient Ceylon, 1909.

Ancient Ayurvedic instruments - Koggala

Aralu, Bulu, Nelli

Here are professed Physicians but all in general have some skill that way and are Physicians to themselves. The woods are the Apothecaries shops, where with herbs, leaves and rind of trees they make all their Physic and plasters with which they do notable cures.

– Robert Knox, 1681.

Elephant treated with native medicine

"Bring me the herbs for which the east is famed".
- Aristotle to Alexander

Scrubbing Stone

Bathers

The essence of village life is community. The values of communal contentment and sharing override the demands of individualism and possession. The activities around the village well - a leisurely meeting place at all times - provide a simple, if significant, symbol of togetherness. The stone used for scrubbing one's body while bathing is never owned as such - it is always left for the next person at the well to use.

- H. A. I. Goonetileke, 1996

Negombo

An Indian Prayer

O' Great Spirit
Let me walk in beauty, and make my eyes ever behold the red and purple sunset.
Make my hands respect the things you have made and my ears sharp to hear your voice.
Make me wise so that I may understand the things you have taught my people.
Let me learn the lessons you have hidden in every leaf and rock.
I seek strength, not to be greater than my brother, but to fight my greatest enemy - myself.
Make me always ready to come to you with clean hands and straight eyes.
Oh Great Spirit whose voice I hear in the winds
Whose breath gives life to the world, hear me,
I come to you as one of your many children
I am small and weak
I need your strength and your wisdom
May I walk in beauty
Make my eyes behold the red and purple sunset
And my ears sharp to your voice
Make me wise so that I may know
The things you have taught your children
The lessons you have written in every leaf and rock
Make me strong, not to be superior to my brothers
But to fight my greatest enemy - myself
Make me ever ready to come to you with straight eyes
So that when life fades, as the fading sunset
My spirit may come to you without shame.

- Chief Dan George

Maga Salakuna

(A pilgrims progress from Badulla to Kandy)

This anonymous Sinhala poem of 203 stanzas in the classical mode may be ascribed from internal and stylistic evidence to the early 17th century. The title of the poem means an itinerary, familiar to readers from the well-known Sandesa (or Messenger poems), like the Kokila, Mayura or Selalihini. Maga Salakuna, however, is a descriptive road guide to a pious pilgrim making a journey from Badulla to the Dalada Maligawa in Kandy. No Sandesa has covered this particular route. Many of the places mentioned can be traced and identified, and the three most important cities of the hill country at the time - Badulupura (Badulla), Diyatilakapura (Diyatilaka or Hanguranketa) and Sirivardhanapura (Kandy). The author has a special feel for topography as well as the entrancing description of scenery, people, flora and fauna. The text used here is based on the translation by Dr. Edmund Peiris, O.M.I., Bishop of Chilaw and M. E. Fernando of 1947. This unique palm leaf manuscript of 17 folios was found in the Hugh Nevill Collection of the British Museum by Bishop Peiris in 1936. Selected verses from this singular poem in the entire corpus of Sinhala literature have been included for illustration, because they serve as a pictorial vehicle for conveying in graphic and moving fashion the essential ingredients of a traditional pilgrimage. This form of excursion partaking of both secular and religious relaxation and devotion was part and parcel of village life. After the tedious and time-honoured cycles of rural agriculture of communities rooted in the soil, such corporate journeyings provided a welcome relief, in the form of discovering picturesque terrain ending in a fabled shrine to the Buddha. Strengthened and refreshed the pilgrims returned home to face the daily round in elevated mood.

- H. A. I. Goonetileke

The Maga Salakuna

Ascription of Worship

1.

Worshipping the feet of Laksmi, Sarasvati,
Of Brahma, Guru, Vinayaka, their favour invoked,
With rhyme and reason, from rhetoric, soul's cheer,
Weaving skilled verses, for the mind's discernment,
I sing the MAGA SALAKUNA.

17.
Displaying the delicate sheen of pretty teeth,
With scanty locks gathered up at the crest,
Like golden sprouts the tender maids with zest
Sport: 'tis hard to pass such scenes unseen.

The Journey Begins

24.

Dispelling the shades of darkness to the nether woods
Awakening every lotus flower from its slumbers deep,
Illuminating the world around with its gladsome rays,
The dazzling sun ascends the summits of the orient hill.

25.
Now leave your abode and cleanse yourself,
Take in your hands such offerings meet,
As perfumes, incense, flowers and lights.
Recall to mind the Sage's goodness,
Invoke your god and fix your gaze
On auspicious signs of route ahead.

27.

Placing your hands upon your head with heart replete with joy,
On your face and hands and knees worship the Mutiyangana.
Where the ascetic's relics are laid with merit accumulated,
To rear undaunted a golden ladder reaching up to the skies.

30.
Observe friend, the little maids frisk upon the strand,
Slipping garments off their shoulders, they hold them in their hand,
Their bodies soiled entire with dust by rolling on the sand
While they prattle snatches of song with many a pleasant jest.

31.
See the bazaars on either side of the well-decked street,
Where eager women squat and heap their wares in neat array,
Cocoanut and oil and rice and fruit, luscious and not a few,
Intent on winning large profits by selling petty stuff.

36.
With pitchers full perched on their hips,
Their lips dyed crimson, like parrot beaks,
Their ample bosoms draped in cloth,
See the fair ones go by with side-long looks.

40.

In days of yore a monarch dwelt in this revered city;
He was like the diadem placed on the crown of the solar race
To mount his elephant, horse and car, as was wont, he placed,
This seemly moon-stone. View it as you go along your way.

42.
Troops of monkeys chattering loud
Hop about the tree-tops.
Down they fling the tender leaves
To the foot of trees before you.
No qualms of fear the scene arouse.
Lo, to your right the royal gardens.

52.
There on your right is the blissful *Bogoda vehera*;
Day and night alike it shines with steady glow
Thrown up from golden minarets of roofs of many houses,
Worship with joy on your way to attain endless happiness.

55.

Beautiful birds perched on tree-tops warble
songs,
Rich, mellow and sweet, they sing the live-long
day.
Hear them, friend, till ears are full and joy
abound,
And rest from journey's toils at *Dambéruppe*.

59.
Numerous fishes great and precious
Dash at all and fight in sport;
Popping in and out they gambol.
Scan them, friend, and bathe yourself in
Sihilpankandura.

61.
Many herds of buffaloes rush on every side,
In defiance they furrow, with hoofs throw up the soil;
In fury they charge with horns and bright sparks emit.
View such scenes with calm, in *Manavela*, my friend.

64.
Now traverse Haltota with a joyous mind,
Where long-eyed females do leisurely watch
For fishes to snatch them on leaving water,
Lullo and petio, tying them with dul strand.

67.
Notice my friend before proceeding
The Moors at the caravan halting place.
They seize stray oxen, muzzle them fast,
Twisting their tails load them heavily
And draw down sin. Their merchandise is
In pots and pans and salt and dry fish.

The Forest Scene

71.
Espy, my friend beloved, on your way
The wild Veddahs who shout aloud as they cast
Their seines and hedge in on every side,
Standing at intervals in the thickets there.

72. Wild buffaloes with hoofs scatter the entire soil,
They rush about the woods and engage in strife;
Bright sparks splash from their rigid horns.
'Tis good to see them with a stout heart.

73.
Haste gladly, friend, though hair stands on end,
Listening with apathy, but with ears intent,
To the drone of bees which among thriving foliage
Of furze and fern, murmur here and there.

74.
Gaze on the charm of picturesque forest trees,
Nika and *Kinihira, Karamba* and *Ratamba,*
Para, Hora and *Ebony, Mango, Domba* and *Giramba,*
Mandara and *Bijupura, Samandara* and *Polamba.*

75.
Harken, my good friend, as merrily you go
To praying hermits, who keep the full precepts,
To coveys of peacocks, strutting and shrieking
On crags, and mosquitoes buzzing high and low.

76.
There in the forest in diverse places
Are herds of deer, which resting or grazing,
Prick up their ears and flee away scared.
See them, my pal, and continue your journey.

89.
Rejoice at the sight of the *kindura* maidens,
Their brows with vermilion *tilaka* adorned,
Their tresses bedecked with peacock plumes,
Blowing oaten flutes and horns in accord.

90.
With matted locks loosened on the neck
And bulging bellies big as pots,
Wild women squat by trees and stare
With their babes. Away from them.

86.
Fail not to observe the flights of wild birds
Perched on branches with their young mates;
With beaks they make their fledglings comely
And blow reedy notes in songs melodious.

87.
When elks in strife lock their horns sparks fly about;
By honour urged they take to the woods terror-stricken,
With their young offspring and dear mates they wander
At their sight stray not far but haste away.

91.
Blue-necked peacocks dance on craggy knolls,
With gaudy tail-plumes spread in ten directions,
'Mid charming peahens, with passionate
gladness
Gloating in the sun with long-drawn cries.

92.
Direct your sight to the elephants, my friend,
Which stretch out their trunks to bend the twigs,
And scatter on the path, eating them greedily,
While their dams and calves receive their share.

104.
Elephants from the woods emerge herd by herd,
They dig up plantain for repast, bush by bush,
And face in battle, emitting sparks, tusk to tusk.
View them, friend, there they are in the patana.

110.
Be pleased at the sight of Veddah women, a cloth about their loins,
Their sucklings fastened to their waist, their matted locks wound tight
To a knot upon their head; they are seen in the forest depths.
Now direct your course, my friend, over *Dandubandiruppe*.

153.
A woman takes water into her open palm,
Sees her face there and fancies it were a flower,
Thoughtlessly she says it to her fair gossip,
Then parts her palms at once with a laugh.

160.
The splash of water thrown by a wench
Settled on the bosom at the tip of the breast.
It blossomed like a lotus on the beak of a swan;
Many were the women who hastened in that belief.

161.
Some plunge into the river and swim,
Some encounter others in the stream,
Some agitate the flood in their course,
Some dive in and part the water in twain.

187.
Friend, with subdued eyes and heart discern
On your left the iron-smiths' forge,
Where with many a sledge-hammer stroke
They scatter steadily sparks in showers.

194.
'Tis hard to turn away your gaze from pleasing
maids,
With dark bright eyes, anointed for distinction,
Their cygnet-like breasts set full on their
bosoms,
In form as graceful as the consort of Visnu.

Dalada Maligawa

203.
After contemplating with joy the bliss of this Metropolis
Where the sky is a mass of lustre from sparkling gems,
The abode of noble kings of the famous solar race,
Enter, my friend, with satisfaction the *Dalada Maligava*.

VI. An enduring chant for survival

Polonnaruwa

Dreams from Six Worlds Apart

By **Pradeep Prabhu**

Abbreviated from *Down to Earth*, August 15, 1995

We have been told till today that the white men, and after they went away, the brown men with white masks, always want the correct things, and when they want our "development", it is also the correct thing. We fear, however, that their kind of development will destroy our land, our culture, our traditions, history, ethos and ways of life. We are forced to "desire" their kind of development because it is supposed to ensure for us a better future. But we have no future . . . only a past. Not even a present. We are born old and we die young, and we try to remain awake in other peoples dreams.

Today you are saying that sustainable development is what the earth needs, and we feel it is what mother nature wants ... only, we are often unable to hear her. We rub our eyes in disbelief because now, suddenly, we are hearing from you what our elders have always said. We were almost beginning to forget their wisdom, and most of our children, particularly those educated in the schools of white men, have already forgotten these.

We are happy that you can now dream of sustainable, eco-friendly development. Only, we have forgotten how to dream, because from dream we have to wake up to a reality that is painful.

We are sorry that we sound pessimistic. We don't wish to discourage you, because what you

◀ *Ehetuwewa*

now seek, we have always believed to be right. We share our pain with you because you have hope, and we hope to be able to once again hope with you. We try to communicate in the hope that what we share may make sense to you even though it is from a different civilization. And we know you will try to understand.

So we are also afraid of being robbed of our home and hearth. Our elders say that when the white men came, six generations ago, we suddenly became "thieves" and "thugs", and unwanted in the forests which were till then our homes, because they said that from then on it belonged to them and we became their serfs.

We now hear about the World Bank and the International Monetary Fund and how they are eager to lead this country to the future prosperity of the "free market". But we are thinking of what happens to the third world within the Third World: it is the process of internal colonization . . . white men come from across the seas to satisfy their greed, and tell us that it is *our* need.

Anyway, since you have begun to think of the extent to which mother earth can bear with our abuse, we feel it is necessary to share some of our own beliefs about her and her varied offspring which you classify as flora, fauna and humans.

We believe that we cannot own mother earth, we can only partake of her bounty, which is more plentiful than all the products of our labours. Hence, we celebrate nature and her bounty each time we can begin our work in the fields. We believe that only one part of her bounty is land, but it cannot belong to us, humans, exclusively. On the contrary, it is we who belong to the land.

But we are sad for ourselves because we have always believed in what you have now begun to believe, and yet all around we are being made to look like fools and being taught that our ancestors thought like fools, and therefore made no progress. And if we are to make progress, then we should walk the way of the world, give up our "narrow" outlook, stop being toads in the well and work hard to produce more, accumulate

Gongala

Bagura

Dune Water - Udappuwa

Pusulpitiya

more, consume more, and have the best that your modernity has to offer, that is, things, more things and still more things.

We are sad that our way of life, our ethos, spirituality, morality and simplicity is coming under relentless attack, which only intensifies with each passing hour. We are sad that more and more of us are getting confused and we are losing our battles. Our younger people are moving further and further from us with each passing generation. And we are worried that we will have no opportunity to pass on the sceptre to a new generation. So what you say is like a breath of fresh air. It gives some of us a faint ray of hope. We want you very much to succeed.

Good-bye, friends. Please don't stop dreaming. Although your dreams may appear today to be at the far side of the rainbow, we will be happy to be a part of your dreams.

Thimbulketiya
Jaffna

Ehetuwewa

Katnoruwa

Hill Country
Dumbara Valley

Udappu

Tangalle

Balaluwewa

Negombo

Anuradhapura

◂ *Nagrak*

Vessagiriya

Vessagiriya

Ehetuwewa

Old Village - Sasseruwa

Kandy

Batalagoda

Ehetuwewa

Manikkapola Uttu -Wilpattu

VII. This is a heritage that ever lives

Anuradhapura

From the moment on June 28th, 1820 that Lt. M. H. Fagan of His Majesty's Second Ceylon Regiment stumbled on the "ancient ruins and colossal figures" at Polonnaruva (then known to the recently arrived British as Topary, a corruption derived from Topawewa, a tank in the vicinity) while marching from Batticaloa to Minneriya with a detachment of troops during the dying days of the Kandyan Rebellion of 1818, the Holy Cities of Ceylon and their Buddhist monuments have remained in the limelight of antiquarian research and popular interest. This happy discovery of Ceylon's second great capital was soon matched by the equally accidental revelation to British eyes of Anuradhapura and Mihintale when Ralph Backhouse, Collector of Mannar, described the ruined glories of the earlier Raja Rata (the Land of the Kings).

These twin centres of Sinhala hegemony were abandoned to the enveloping jungle when successive floodtides of South Indian invasion and the collapse of its hydraulic civilization accompanied inexorably by the rapid decline of the congenial and prosperous modes of production and ravaging disease, had compelled the inglorious retreat of a once-proud society to the constricted security and enfeebling confines of the central hills. The new kingdom was a valiant, resourceful and decorative, though parvenu, successor to the stupendous splendours of Anuradhapura and Polonnaruva which had lasted from first establishment in the 4th century BC for nearly one thousand seven hundred years of illustrious history.

The systematic, though far from comprehensive, excavations and restorations by the Archaeological Survey of Ceylon since the eighteen seventies have uncovered from the debris of centuries and the invincible deluge of the ravishing jungle a whole corpus of architectural glory and achievement for the enchantment and wonder of the humdrum twentieth century visitor to these green abodes of the haunting gods. To the pious indigene, however, the appeal and power of these religious monumens had remained essentially undiminished despite cloistered remoteness and the disfiguring desolation of disrespectful time. It was on alien student and foreign visitor that they were to exert a compelling attraction and unrestrained charm as conveying the distinctive character and way of life, as well as the characteristic ecology of an enduring civilisation.

All through the ages the spectacle of ancient monuments has afforded various kinds of pleasure and excitement to people, and the beauty, picturesqueness and exotic quality of diverse ruins have been a potent ingredient in wanderlust. In the last hundred years, particularly, when the arts and crafts of travel began to boom, the ruined cities of the East have served as a durable fascination for every European visitor. The pages of travel literature are littered with rhapsodies on the decayed grandeurs of the fabled past and few travellers have failed to be enthralled by the mute and melancholy magnificence of prostrate architectural sublimity. The most banal, commonplace or pedestrian tourist cannot fail to be uplifted even temporarily by the sudden sight of these ghostly halls and serene sculptures, even though he may have choked over the captivating taradiddles and mendacities of Tourist Board folklore. The ruins of Ceylon have their firm and perennial place in the lasting catalogue of Asia's historic treasures, and scores of books and hundreds of articles have sung their praise in terms of poetic intoxication and romantic fervour verging on the seductively imprecise. But each visitor brings to his or her account that special blend of excitement and fantasy, which weaves its own particular spell over the reader.

- H. A. I. Goonetileke, *Lanka, their Lanka*, 1984.

Dandhabanavaka

(from a bas-relief, 10th century)

Enclosed world: in its duplicity
It is drawn with long red female hair
Over a glaring lake;
Its carved wings flutter in disused time -
Its feet are caught in a staircase of branches -
In a ruched spiral, or a
Monstrous climbing eye.

- Lakdasa Wikkramasinha, *Nossa Senhora Dos Chingalas, Poems 1965-1970*, 1973.

Mihintale

Tivanka Pillimage - Polonnaruwa

Tivanka Pillimage - Polonnaruwa

With many the joints are broken and their pinnacles destroyed, with others the roofs have decayed and the bricks are broken. Only walls and pillars remain. In others again the gates have fallen in and the hinging of the gate-posts destroyed; in others again the steps have become loosened and the railings have fallen in. Of many all that can be seen are parts still hanging together from the original foundation wall. Of many not even the place where they once stood is now to be seen. Of what use are many words. This town which has once lost all its glory we shall again make glorious.

- A. Liyanagamage,
The Decline of Polonnaruwa, 1968.

Wijerama - Anuradhapura

Wijerama - Anuradhapura

But the Vijayarama was worth the ride. It is quite magnificent, especially the never-roofed hall with its bas-reliefs: it is also exceptionally interesting as a complete establishment, with dagaba and shrine-room and monks' quarters and even a hot-air bath. It has no history; it was "heretical", Mahayanist, and probably even Tantric, a debased School mixing magic and sexual rites into Buddhism. It seems to date from about the same period as the Western Monasteries, when Mahayanism was tending to eclipse the orthodox School.

- R. Raven Hart,
Ceylon : History in Stone, 1964

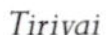

Tiriyai

At Tiriyai, there is a vatadage located on a hill to the west of the village. A flight of steps leads to the summit, which has been levelled to build a small dagaba on it. Later it was enlarged, and about the 8th century A.D., encircled by a vatadage. There are two concentric circles of pillars round the dagaba and at the edge of the dagaba platform is a stone screen wall about 6 feet high with holes at intervals for pillars. Other objects of interest are a pre-Christian inscription in a cave on the hill, an 8th century Sanskrit inscription on a boulder and remains of an image house.

- *Handbook for the Ceylon Traveller*, 2nd ed., Studio Times, 1983.

Ochappu Kallu - Wilpattu

OCHAPPU KALLU, some 8 miles or more inland from Kudramalai, the Hipporos of Pliny, is identified as the Acha Nagara mentioned in the inscription at Tonigala. "The horse city would naturally be about that distance inland from its port at the horse point. With *acha* for *asa*, horse, compare the variants Chola and Sola. There would be reason for this tenure under the temple of the Achagiriya Tisa Pawata (which Nevill identifies with Paramakanda), because it would naturally be the port of disembarkation of pilgrims to that shrine from India, a pilgrimage kept up till recent times." (*Taprobanian*, 7).

"About 5 or 6 miles south of the Modragam-ar, or Sandanan-purawetiyaoya, are extensive remains of a temple, in the centre of which are two remarkable rocks called *Ochayappukallu*, the leaning stone. These rocks are on the summit of a hill and appear as if they had originally been perpendicular, but had by some accident fallen one over the other, and being arrested in their descent half way by smaller fragments beneath and between them, lie with one elevated at a considerable angle from the ground. It is difficult even to conjecture how these masses of rock ever got into this position. They are, I think, as large as, if not longer than the cromleches at Stonehenge. Surrounding these rocks in every direction are circles of pillars as at Nugil-ar and Tammana Nuwara in various stages of preservation: some upright, some lying flat, with other stones of various shapes roughly hewn or simply carved, all denoting the site of an extensive edifice. At the foot of the elevated ground on which these ruins stand, working towards the south, is a ravine between perpendicular cliffs which forms the basin of a beautiful tank. The reservoir is faced with a rich grassy slope on the higher side and closed with a substantial earthen mound, on the lower, of such broad and solid dimensions as to render it a matter of doubt whether it is a natural formation or an artificial bund.

- Frank Modder,
Manual of the Puttalam District, 1908.

The Buddha Image by the River

Afraid of getting muddied feet
You turn them up in the lotus position
And directing your mind to the flowing river
You sit there - say are you not sad?

Perched up there on granite rock
What is this path you reveal?
Afraid of muddied feet
Soles upturned
Perched on a rock
What path do you reveal?

Entwined, embracing, stumbling, falling,
Heady lotus scents releasing
Formed of gem-like pebble clusters
This lovely wayward stream keeps flowing
Kissing . . . Kissing . . .

But your two eyes see only
The mud of the river bottom.

Aware that the mud might sully your feet -
Afraid - you abandoned wife and son
Fled in darkness
Leapt the stream
Sought a great black granite cavern
There lifted up the soles of your feet
And assumed the lotus position.
And what is more you now tell us
That we too should climb the rock
Cross our legs with soles turned up
And sit, just looking on.

"Sit upon that granite rock
Look not on the lovely stream
Contemplate its muddy bed
And like me, be still."

- Gunadasa Amerasekera

tr. by Ranjini Obeyesekere. *An Anthology of Modern Writing from Sri Lanka*, 1981, verses 1-7.

Attaragollewa - Bakamuna
Anuradhapura

In the midst of this twined, entrenched woodland, with its separate life of animals, birds, reptiles, insects, plants, rocks, we came to the abandoned kingdoms of Anuradhapura and Polonnaruwa, capitals of the first Sinhalese kings. Their temples had been burst open by vines, trees grew through their thick stone walls. Hidden in a clearing, with langurs whooping round, an immense fractured Buddha lay on his side, sealed eyes calm. At this time the ruins were not as well cared for as they are now: at Sigiriya, a great forested rock on whose summit was a cave full of decayed frescoes, immense brown beehives, like enlarged pinecones, hung by the spiral iron stairway to the top, and the air was full of a sound like the thunder of a distant war. Yet to see these fallen monuments, invaded by the jungle, inhabited by beasts, made me aware of history. They were more alive to me because though the human life in them was dead, another, prehistoric life had taken over. History to me was the way a spindly shoot sprouted through Buddha's stone eye.

- Dom Moraes, *My Son's Father,* 1968.

. . . stone is ancient, not only in the sense that it withstands the wear of time better than other natural things, but also in the sense that its antiquity is of the order of the always already. Stone comes from a past that has never been present, a past unassimilable to the order of time in which things come and go in the human world. . .

- John Sallis,
Stone, 1994.

Mihintale

Polonnaruwa

Anuradhapura Stone Bridge

This picturesque ruin of the ancient bridge one hundred and twenty feet long, and now stretching its gigantic arm only half-way into the river, shorn of all its splendour yet beautiful in its nakedness, flooding our minds with the story of twenty-two centuries ago. What countless processions of pilgrims must have passed over this bridge on their way to holy Mihintale! What haughty kings and gallant princes must have rolled in their chariots along this road in all their pomp and pageantry! How often had the hallowed feet of Arahat Mahinda sanctified these very stones!

- Hubert E. Weerasooriya,
Voices In Stones, 1958.

Stone Bridge - Anuradhapura

Polonnaruwa

Polonnaruwa

After the desertion of Anuradhapura, Polonnaruwa took its place as royal capital. It was abandoned at the end of the thirteenth century; more utterly abandoned, for not even a village marked its site; its ruins lay, and vast numbers of them still lie, unseen in the forest which engulfed them. Pushing through the eighty miles or so of jungle from Anuradhapura along the forest tracks (avoiding the road), is to journey through exotic beauty, strangely set with the half buried ruins of an ecclesiastical Buddhist world – temples and dagobas that sprout with trees, statues and carved sculptures partly seen among the rank undergrowth, groups of monastery buildings in all stages of ruin and clearance, hermitages enclosed in great tangles of twisting tree roots, hung with brilliant flowers and skipped about by monkeys, rock baths, and cisterns and large pools bright with kingfishers and full of tortoises, stone portals carved with Buddhas, elephants and cobras, groups of richly-capitaled pillars, moonstone stair slabs carved with prancing animals, great monasteries of temples and pillars such as Jetawanarama, built two thousand years ago and scattered for miles through the forest, the remains of palaces, rocky hills covered with terraces and steps, grass and scrub, and finally Polonnaruwa on its lake, with the great pleasure garden the Park of Heaven, laid out by King Parakrama in the twelfth century. This must have been a glorious landscape park, set with lotus-grown pools, a dazzling and exquisite bathing hall with sandalwood pillars, a summer pavilion, a royal palace of great loveliness. All this is described in the Mahawansa in enthusiastic and beautiful detail; we can see the ruins of each thing described, and imagination rears the palace and park as they were.

- Rose Macaulay,
The Pleasure of Ruins, 1953.

I came to the temple of Siva, which stands to the south of the priestly city, and serves to remind us how great and valuable was the influence of South India upon the architecture of Ceylon. As I looked at the grey stone temple I remembered how it stood for centuries in the grip of the jungle, so that trees grew from its very walls, and wild elephants browsed upon the mound of debris under which it was half-buried. When Major Forbes saw it in 1828 he told how "bears in numbers find shelter amongst these ruins, and this sanctuary had only been vacated by some of them hearing the noise of our approach...

- W.T. Keble,
Ceylon Beaten Track. 1940.

Polonnaruwa

Anuradhapura

The sloping face of the rock (a breadth of 32 ft. in all) on either side of this strangely cramped,round-back, chamber has been carved into wondrously realistic bas-reliefs in perfect keeping with the *pokuna*. These represent elephants in a lotus- covered tank. On the rock slope to the right three elephants are shown lazily disporting themselves in the water, indisturbed, amid lotuses and fish. On the left the scene is vividly changed. Some sudden alarm has roused the elephants; one seems to be scenting danger, the other two are already in full flight. This absolutely unique piece of carving is without exception the most spirited and life-like to be seen anywhere among the ruins of Anuradhapura.

- H. C. P. Bell,
A.S.C.A.R., 1901.

Polonnaruwa

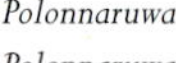

No scene can be conceived more impressive than this beautiful city must have been in its pristine splendour: its stately buildings stretching along the shore of the lake, their gilded cupolas reflected on its still expanse and embowered in the dense foliage of the surrounding forests. At the present day it is by far the most remarkable assemblage of ruins in Ceylon, not alone from the number and dimensions, but from the architectural superiority, of its buildings. Pollanarrua was a place of importance at a very early period, so much so that king Sri Sangabo III, without altogether deserting his capital, made this his favourite residence, and died here A.D. 718. It was to Parakrama Bahu I that Pollanarrua owed the magnificence which is attested by the ruins that survive to the present day.

- Sir James Emerson Tennent,
Ceylon, 1860

Polonnaruwa

Polonnaruwa

Yapahuwa

Polonnaruwa

Polonnaruwa

The staircase in Antiquity

If we examine the dimensions of the steps leading into the peristyles of ancient temples, they will be found to be proportioned to the ordonnance, magnitude and character of the building rather than for ease of ascent. Indeed, we cannot expect to gain much information on this head from the ancients, when it is considered that their buildings, in general, both public and private, consisted of a ground floor only. Staircases are mentioned by Homer, and Lysias in one of his Orations speaks of two storeys, while at Pompeii there is an instance of a house with a second floor; but as Pliny and Varro do not mention staircases in the description of their villas, it is reasonable to conclude that they were of very inconsiderable extent. In modern works, both public and private, staircases are the very touchstone of sound knowledge and real merit in the architect. In every building there are features of such importance that to determine their proper situation, character and extent,as well as their most suitable forms and proper decorations, requires all the experience and judgement of the most able architects.

- Sir John Soames, *Lectures on Architecture*, quoted by Roloff Beny in *Romance of Architecture*, 1985.

Adam's Peak

The Sixth Voyage of Sindbad

Now the Island Sarandib lieth under the equinoctial line, its night and day both numbering twelve hours. It measureth eighty leagues long (approximately 300 miles, though the term may have been used poetically to mean almost any distance) by a breadth of thirty and its width is bounded by a lofty mountain and a deep valley. The mountain (Adam's Peak) is conspicuous from a distance of three days and it containeth many kinds of rubies and other minerals and spice trees of all sorts. The surface is covered with emery wherewith gems are cut and fashioned; diamonds are in its rivers and pearls are in its valley. I ascended that mountain and solaced myself with a view of its marvels which are indescribable. . .

Arabian Nights, 10th Century

Isurumuniya

Three Poems for Isurumuniya

I

Stone, Looms and stirs
And does not move and
Moves,
I am stone and stare my soul into this stone
And see it quiver.

II

Stone, pitted,
Weathered twelve centuries,
These, springing from it
Their gesture perfected -
Passionate exactitude
Of that waking dream
In which line, form
Stirred in the stone, heaved into being, sank
In this abnegation, leaving us
These lovers, not the chisel, not
The man.

III

Poised and tensed
Caught at the hushed weightless point of pause
Tying look to look
Act presaged, imminent, and
In abeyance.

- Ashley Halpe,
Homing and other poems, 1993.

Kalinga Nuwara

The Mahaveli-ganga-the Baracus or Ganges of Ptolemy-has long been eulogized as the "Queen of Lanka's streams". Historical topography of ancient and medieval times refers to it by many names: Ganga or Mahaganga or Mahavaluka Ganga. Emerging from the hills into the lowlands about 7 miles north of Alutnuwara (Mahiyangana) it flows in a north-north-easterly direction to the sea off Trincomalee. The country which lies to the east of Polonnaruva is the flood plain of this river. At least twice each year the surcharged waters overflow the river's banks and fill every depression in the flood plain at each overflow, forming lakelets which are called "vil".

This region is possibly the least known parcel of country to most people in Ceylon. Yet it is a locality full of interest to anybody who has cultivated a "seeing eye" and takes the trouble to give a little of his mind to objects which are linked to history, archaeology or biology. The charm of these vast sheets of marsh and water referred to as Handapan Vila, Bendiya Vila and Gengala Vila and many others which lie scattered north of Manampitiya, is indescribable; the varied bird and animal life, and withal that wondrous hush which pervades and sanctifies these open spaces where Nature is almost uninvaded by man's encroachment. You approach the southern limits of this region from Polonnaruva, making the crossing over the Mahaveli-ganga at Dastota – a ford where history is writ large, and was known by the name Sahassatittha in the past.

Four miles up-river from Dastota there is a small island about a mile long narrowing at its northern end. Around it the river flows with much impetuosity. At one time this *duva* (island) was known as Kalinga Nuwara, and if you have the opportunity to do some "sight-seeing" on it you will find many traces of ruined structures, and evidence of past civilization in masses of brickbats on the surface, and stumps of stone pillars, which indicate that practically the entire island was covered by buildings. You will find simple carved stone *makara* balustrades flanking the entrances to buildings, the foundations of large halls (72 ft. by 51 ft.), seemingly elliptical in shape, circular, low brick-walled enclosures and even the traces of a roadway which runs for about half a mile.

Kalinga Nuwara

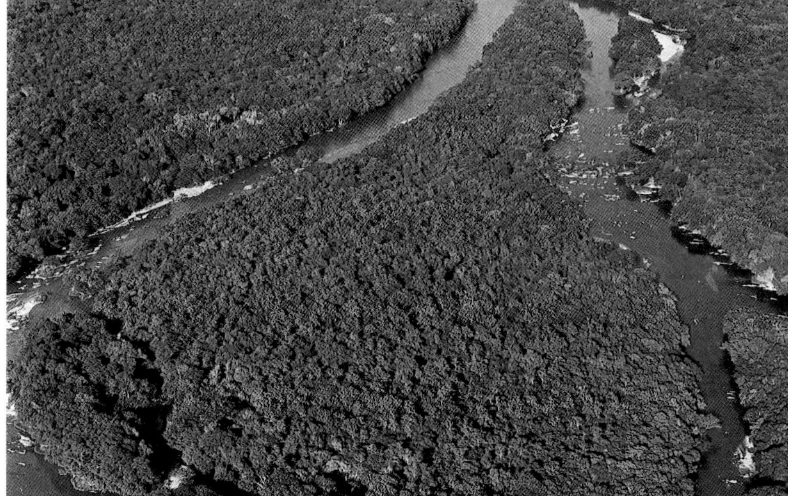

Kalinga Nuwara may well be the historical site where in medieval times the ceremony of the ordination of monks was held. A chapter in the *Mahavamsa*, which we are told was "composed equally for the delight and amazement of good men", refers to one such ordination in the 13th century, when Vijaya Bahu convened the whole of the Buddhist clergy to a "treat" of ordination to do which he sent a prince and "caused him to build many thousands (sic) of beautiful dwelling places for priests and large and lofty halls . . . and sent an invitation by messenger to all parts saying, lo! we are about to hold a feast of Ordination. Now, therefore, such monks as are well disposed towards us-be they great elders, middle elders, or juniors - let them, even all of them, endeavour to come to Sahassatittha".

The many islets off the southern end of the larger island called Kalinga Nuwara divide the Mahaveli-ganga here into seven channels. There is a tradition that near this spot the Sinhalese kings of old had establishments for building galleys and "tsampans". This perhaps bears the stamp of some truth for the section of the river between these islands and the sea off Trincomalee is of sufficient depth at all times to be navigable for small vessels, while moreover the borders of the river bear high forest timbers suitable for boat building.

When Parakramabahu at the height of his power was provoked to declare war against Alaungsithu, the King of Burma, as a result of a series of aggressions culminating with the seizure of a Sinhalese princess on her way to Siam, this spot - we can well imagine - must have been a great ship-building yard. We are not told what was the number of the assemblage of ships which eventually set out on the expedition - but it is written in the *Culavamsa* that only five ships reached the destination and "the troops landed, defeated the Burmese forces who opposed them, and laid waste the surounding country". I cite: "if the *Culavamsa* narrative is construed literally . . . the victories gained by six troop-ships can only be explained either by a lamentable state of unpreparedness for defence in the Burmese Kingdom . . . or is just another laudatory exaggeration of the marvellous power of its heroes' arms".

- R. L. Brohier,
Seeing Ceylon, 2nd ed., 1971.

The Singalese write very neatly and expeditiously, with a sharp-pointed iron style; and, they colour the characters they have scratched by rubbing them with an ink made of lamp-black and a solution of gum. Their books are all manuscript, and actually formed of leaves of trees, and confined by boards. The leaf most used, as best adapted to the purpose, is the immense leaf of the talipot-palm, occasionally nearly thirty feet in circumference. It is well and slowly dried in the shade, rubbed with an oil, and cut into pieces of suitable dimensions, the length of which always greatly exceeds the width; near the two extremities each piece is perforated, that they may be connected by means of a cord, to which the boards also are attached, to form a book. The boards are generally neatly painted and decorated. Occasionally, but rarely, their books are made of thin copper plates.

The materials of their writings are durable, and they last much longer than ours, particularly in Ceylon, where our paper is so apt to be destroyed by insects, and our ink to fade. Their books are pretty numerous, and though much more expensive than our printed works, are very much cheaper than MSS were in Europe before printing was invented.

- John Davy,
An Account of the Interior of Ceylon, 1821.

Peradeniya

Ola-leaf manuscript

An intriguing location was found at Maduru Oya in 1983. "The upstream position of the sluice is a masterpiece of construction. The two conduits with corbetted arches approximately 2.5 metres apart pass through this bund. At the downstream end, a terra-cotta relief depicting dancing figures can be seen in brick, facing the two arches. The dancing figures have been mutilated and the marks of a chisel can be seen on the carved relief."

- *Mahaveli Report,* 1983.

Maduru Oya - Bisokotuwa

Maduru Oya - Bisokotuwa

Tissamaharama

There is no doubt what they are: they have footrests for the squatting user, and a place for his ablutionary water-pot, and between the footrests there is a depression with a drainage-hole. The odd thing about them is that the horizontal slab, and a vertical endpiece towards which the user faced, are elaborately, even flamboyantly carved; and this in monastic buildings which otherwise are austerely unornamented except for very simple mouldings. One can understand the simplicity, since the monks here were as extreme ascetics as the Rule allowed, everting to primitive practice in using for robes only rags picked up from cemeteries and dust-heaps; but why the elaborate lavatories? Perhaps, and for what the suggestion may be worth, these monks thus ornamented their privies to show their contempt for the art and elaborations of the older foundations like the Utopians who showed their contempt for gold by using it only for their chamber-pots.

- R. Raven Hart,
Ceylon : History in Stone, 1964

Anuradhapura

Sasseruwa

Island of Stone

Sri Lanka lies within the blue expanse of the Indian Ocean. It is divided from India by a shallow strait less than 40 kilometers wide. The island therefore has the same solid continental floor of gneiss and slate as Southern India. During the various geological eras, the island disappeared beneath the sea, to rise again at a later stage. During the late Tertiary period, the land was covered with a thick layer of limestone. Movement in the earth's crust and continual erosion exposed both young and old stone: crystalline limestone, black, grey and pink granite, greenstone, striated gneiss, and sandstone in many earthy shades.

In these stones and rock faces the architects of ancient royal cities, the builders and stone masons of many temples, the authors of inscriptions and the carvers of sculptures and reliefs all found the material which would lend eternal eloquence to their work.

- W. G. M. Beumer,
Studio Times Exhibition *'Eloquence in Stone'*,
1995, Amsterdam.

Polonnaruwa

The successive stages lead through the phenomenal and human world which the Buddha saw as being continually aflame with the fires of craving - the outermost band with the tongues of flame; through the cycle of the four perils which beset all existence - the four animals on the next band signifying birth (elephant) decay (bull), disease (lion) and death (horse); the creeper of desire - the scroll with the undulating design of leaves and flowers, the state of existence in which discrimination is attained, signified by the *hamsa* (goose) with its ability to separate the good from the bad, as it was one of the mythical abilities of this bird to drink the milk in a mixture of milk and water, and to leave the water behind; through a further stage, signified by the waterlilies, of desire brought under control, and then to the central lotus signifying 'firm establishment among the possibilities of existence', or 'birth and manifestation primarily in the intelligible, or also and consequently in the sensible, world'.

- E. F. C. Ludowyk,
The Footprint of the Buddha, 1958.

Nillakgama

Of the original enclosure for the Bodhi-tree-the *Bodhi-ghara* - at Anuradhapura nothing now survives. The tree, probably the oldest historical tree of which record is extant, is still there, surrounded by a modern structure of a distressing ugliness. Vogel writing more than twenty years ago commented on the difficulty at the present time of mediating between the claims of the zeal of the devout and the demands of an aesthetic sensibility. It is pleasant to record in this connection the work of the Archaeological Department of Ceylon; it has been noteworthy in the care of its restoration, and its resistance to the misguided enthusiasm so often accompanied by bad taste. What that ancient *Bodhi-ghara* must have looked like has recently been revealed in the beautiful restoration of the only one so far discovered in Ceylon - at Nillakgama in the Kurunegala district, not far from Galgamuwa and Maho.

This handsome example of eighth or ninth-century work, perhaps the site of one of the saplings of the original branch, demonstrates how strong and true both the architectural and sculptural traditions of the Sinhalese were. The square enclosure to which two entrances are provided – east and west – is of moulded stone with a frieze of elephants running round the base at the level of the landing. The door-jambs and lintels are ornamented. Inside, on a raised platform in the centre, also ornamented, are lions carved on the vertical slabs which must have surrounded the tree. The four altars on the four sides indicate the presence of the specific object of worship.

As one comes upon this chaste and modest structure, not far from the village tank in the jungle, its yellowish stone - an effect which its long burial under-ground may have produced - is the first intimation of its unusualness. The linear rhythm of the walls with their moulding and the coping is relieved by the sweep of the carving – the creeper on the door-way, the naga-king with his multiple hoods, and the cherub bestriding a horse. The simple dignity of the lions on the vertical slabs of the upper platform is in keeping with the general restraint of the whole structure. The elaborate ornament on the door-frames is not felt to be excessive, it is held in poise by the gravity of the lines of the stone-faced wall and the upper platform.

Of this beautifully integrated work of art Dr. Paranavitane writes: 'In its ornamental character, the structure at Nillakgama is not surpassed by any other monument at the *prasadas* of Anuradhapura. No door-frames so elaborately ornamented as those at Nillakgama are known from any other site as early as the ninth century. A structure on which so much of artistic effort was lavished must have been dedicated to an object of great religious veneration. It is not impossible that the Bodhi-tree which stood at the centre of the upper platform was one believed to have sprung from the seeds of the Anuradhapura Bodhi-tree immediately after it was planted in the reign of Devanampiya Tissa.'

- E. F. C. Ludowyk,
The Footprint of the Buddha, 1958.

Anuradhapura

For Anuradhapura was a great city from the fifth century B.C. to the ninth A.D., when the turbulent Tamils invaded and caused it to be abandoned. What has chiefly so far been reclaimed from the jungle is the monastic settlement. Those great assemblages of pillars, the storied Mahawansa, the humped dagobas, are not excessively beautiful in themselves, in spite of carved moon-shaped stone slabs, sculptured Buddhas and elephants; what gives them aesthetic charm is their situation, jungle-surrounded, barely reclaimed, the green sward on which they stand, the scattered lakes, the delicious stone baths, the clammy, swooning climate which lies like warm, scented flowers on forest and clearing, the frisking monkeys, and, above all, the long reaches of the mysterious, exotic past, winding like a dimly seen river through green enjungled silence to the gorgeous heyday of royal and priestly magnificence of two thousand years ago, and beyond that to the earliest beginnings when the bo-tree took root.

- Rose Macaulay,
The Pleasure of Ruins, 1953.

Polonnaruwa

Yet in Ceylon, I have no doubt that an antiquary can have as ample a field of research or speculation, amidst its numerous and surprising ruins, and its remaining stupendous works, achieved by its ancient inhabitants, that he may hear as many legendary or traditional tales connected with them, as in any other part of the world.

- James Campbell,
Excursions, adventures and field-sports in Ceylon, 1843.

One of the loveliest things to be seen is the Lotus bath - five granite flower-shaped circular steps, lying one within the other, until they enclose the rose-shaped bath itself. Such carved decoration as there is (the colossal Buddhas, the charming elephants, the naive stone dwarfs that guard the sacred places, the animals and flowers) has an engaging Cingalese grace, in keeping with the swinging bells and the scented flowers. You will not encounter in Ceylon those barbaric winged bulls and lions and bearded ox-eyed men of Assyria; the sculptured youths have long painted almond eyes and delicate hands. These de-forested ruins of ancient Buddhism lack the finest architecture and art, but they have much compensating charm.

- Rose Macaulay,
The Pleasure of Ruins, 1953

Polonnaruwa

Nalanda

Polonnaruwa

Words fail altogether to give an idea of the daintiness and originality of the details which mark this architectural monument. The idea of the lotus flower runs through it all. The cone-shaped heads of the posts are the exact shape of those unopened buds, which, to this day, are offered for sale in piles outside every shrine. The head of each pillar standing on the inner platform originally showed carving representing an opening lotus. Some of these still remain. It may be remarked as strange that countries so widely, different in climate and conditions as Ceylon and Egypt, the one so richly moist and the other so curiously dry, each relied so much on the same flower, the lotus, for their conventional ornament in architecture.

Here we may trace the lotus everywhere, in copings, on the heart of moonstones, on pillars and panels. In Egypt more than half the capitals of the mighty columns show symbolic representations of this flower.

It seems possible that the vainglorious Nissanka was really the originator of this famous altar with which his name is for ever associated, for inscriptions on the coping and pillar fragments definitely proclaim it to be so.

The resetting of the posts and pillars, the refitting of the broken fragments so as once again to reveal this flower-shrine as it was, has been a labour requiring infinite patience, but the result is well worth it. It is safe to say that even if all other of the Polonnaruwa monuments eventually fade from the memory of those who have seen them, the Floral Altar and Wata-dage can never be forgotten.

- G. E. Mitton, *The Lost Cities of Ceylon*, 1916.

Pulligoda: Three and half miles to the south of Dimbulagala are ancient paintings in a cave on a boulder. Two layers of plaster of clay and of lime have been applied on the rock face to prepare it for the painting, which depicts five gods seated on a beautifully embroidered scarf-four in the *anjali mudra* (making obeisance with palms together) and the fifth holds up a garland of flowers. Part of the painting which probably belongs to the 12th century, has broken off.

- *Handbook for the Ceylon Traveller,*
2nd ed., Studio Times, 1983.

Pulligoda

But it was especially to see the paintings that I had come to visit the Demala Maha Seya. I passed between the great towering pillars at the entrance into the peace of the sanctuary, where the fallen roof now lets in the daylight and shows the superb dignity of the huge brick statue of the Buddha. Upon the walls on either hand were the paintings of the Jataka stories telling of the former existences of Gautama before he attained Buddhahood. Among them I looked for pictures of men and things as they used to be in Polonnaruwa about 1200 A.D.. On the left hand wall I found a chariot drawn by a horse and painted in yellow and red. The driver perhaps was an ordinary citizen of the ancient town. He was clad in simple waist cloth, beardless, with bracelets upon his arms above the elbows; the lobes of his ears were drawn down to his shoulders according to the ancient custom; his hair seemed to be worn short and his feet were bare. Near him was an archer who had just let fly an arrow. His appearance was just the same as the other.

- W.T. Keble,
Ceylon Beaten Track. 1940.

Polonnaruwa

Sigiriya
Sigiriya

Never a capital, and not even a town or a temple, Sigiriya is the most romantically interesting place in Ceylon. No word exists to describe it properly. It is too small to be called a mountain, too steeply rugged for a hill and too enormous for 'rock' or 'boulder' to suggest it. 'Monolith' is often used, but its connotation is too closely allied with stone worked by man. Sigiriya's formation is entirely natural, its carvings, paintings and architecture being no more than so much added embroidery.

- Vinton Liddell Pickens, *Serendipity*, 1964

Mihintale

That Was

That was an innocent country:
Warlock and dwarf, the hairy forest, dragons
Somewhere there, they said,
Though never seen, sometimes heard:
Somewhere in the hills, the hermit's cavern
Where all was forgiven.

There dying would only be the trek to sleep
Or waking through tall mirrors of a dream:
In spite of which all were afraid to die.

The golden princess had no remedy
When the dragon arrived
But to surrender to his lechery.

Opened her eyes but found herself awake
Or asleep perhaps in the same
Dream by the sleeping unsuffering lake
Where her grief as simple as dying
Pressed her body into the shape of a tear
Lying by embroidered leaves
To fade upon the handkerchiefs of water.
That tyrant was limpid.

With his iron guard of poets and his liars,
He bubbled through stone-walled halls of life
Sucking upon his tide
Like tiny coloured pebbles, chilled desires.

At a river's end
Streams gulp and sweat, expiring in the sand.

- Dom Moraes,
A Beginnning, 1957.

Kayts

It is on these wind-blown, sun-drenched, flat grassy plains that wild ponies roam. There are ample grazing grounds during the rainy season from October to May, and dry grass during the drought. Delft ponies, run wild but are privately owned, lassoed and branded by the owners. They come from a breeding stock maintained from Dutch, and possibly Portuguese times.

The shore line of this island, is unique in that coral rock stands out on the beach and out at sea above the water, having peculiar and fantastic formations. The beach is clean, and the waters are placid and shallow. This is an unspoiled area, where the cries of sea birds, neighing of ponies, mooing of cattle, bleating of goats, the boom of the surf and the gentle whisper of the wind could all be heard.

- *Handbook for the Ceylon Traveller,* 2nd ed., Studio Times, 1983.

Delft

Kayts

There are smaller forts, one by the lagoon at Elephant Pass and two at Kayts (including Fort Hammenhiel). The latter is on an island and is only accessible by boat. It is named 'Heel-of-the-Ham' which the Dutch thought Lanka resembled. There are three large and inhabited islands accessible by cause ways -Kayts, Karaitivu and Pungudutivu. The drive to Kayts in the evening is rewarding for the beautiful sunset it affords. The austere palmyrah palms stand silhouetted against the glorious sky. Kayts, according to legend, is said to be the place from which one of the three Magi came bearing gifts for the infant Jesus.

- *Handbook for the Ceylon Traveller,* 2nd ed., Studio Times, 1983.

Jaffna

Jaffna

Jaffna

Jaffna

The Magnetic North is how someone described that little peninsula called Jaffna at the northern tip of the mango-shaped island of Sri Lanka. This magnetism is no mere flight of poetic fancy. Despite the many attractions in other parts of the country that tempt the visitor to Sri Lanka, Jaffna offers an uniqueness that is hard to define and harder to resist.

Scenic beauty and places of interest Jaffna has in abundance. It has a relatively warmer climate than the rest of the Island, golden beaches and places of historical and religious interest. But people are important, too, for it is people who give character to a place. And Jaffna, a constantly fascinating land, has a character that has been touched but hardly changed by foreign influences, that has been moulded by the harsh climate, and by the protean Hindu religion, its mythology and legend.

- *Handbook for the Ceylon Traveller,*
2nd ed., 1983.

Nallur Kovil - Jaffna

Kandy

Kandy

The Drummer enters the comic play

Having taken drink to get drunk,
With drum slung over the shoulders,
A-tremble all the time,
Then the herald-drummer comes.

In one hand the walking stick,
With drum slung over the shoulders,
From village to village going
Announcing the king's order.

Betel-leaf bag in waist-fold,
Waist in red calico,
Head bound in a turban-
Dressed ready for the crowd.

To announce with the drum,
With drum slung over the shoulders,
Having eaten and drunk, and drunken,
Come, drummer, to the royal crowd!

With palm-leaf sunshade in armpit, and
walking stick in the hand,
With drum, also, tied from the shoulders, and
waist in red calico,
Pausing at times and poking out the beard at
the crowd,
Tremblingly, like an old man, coming into the
crowd.

With walking stick in the hand and palm-leaf
sunshade
With waist in red calico and drum slung over
the shoulder,
Drunken and bowing and bowing to everyone
around in the crowd!

Drunken, having taken toddy, trembling and
stumbling in places,
Raising the eyebrows and shaking the beard at
the crowd,
From the moment it began the drumming
faultily done,
If it goes on thus the herald-drummer will
leave the crowd with a beating!

- tr. by George Keyt,
Poetry from the Sinhalese, 1938.

For Vajira, Dancing

Moving in a lit circle of your own pleasure
quivering precision of hand and arched foot
melting into surprised, unexpected delight
as the arrow, finding it, delights the target,

unconscious of our gaze, arrogant in your careless
spurning of our applause
streaming to you out of the darkness,
conscious if at all only of the drums

sounding beside you, building the stair
up which you sweep, the pedestal
on which you momentarily pause,
the arena in which you aim your javelin glances,

you are for us the essence of poetry
weaving a seamless garment with a housewife's skill
in which the patient stitches disappear
and reappear as one, bright, single

sheet of light to clothe a goddess
or a child: here power and innocence
float into one, as lifted on the beat
of drums, poetry dances on bare feet.

- Yasmine Gooneratne,
New Ceylon Writing, 1971.
Reprinted from *Hemisphere*, 1971

Kandy

Every man has poetry within him. Poetry is the awareness of the mind to the universe. It embraces everything in the world. Of poetry are born religions, philosophies, the sense of good and evil the desire to fight diseases and ignorance and the desire to better matter and mind. Poetry is universal. Poetry is not individual. It exists as a whole in the universal mind. No man is small enough to be disregarded as a poet.

- Meary James Tambimuttu,
Poetry London, 1, 1939

Kandy

Kandy

Kandy

When the Esala moon beckons in the late July or early August, the city of old lives again as the festival most beloved of the Sinhala Buddhists, the Perehera, one of the most magnificent torch-light spectacles anywhere in the world, takes to the streets of Kandy.
The town of Kandy itself puts on a bewitching face as the floodlit Maligawa and the twinkling lights of homes on the hill-slopes are reflected on the waters of the lake against the sombre, mystical darkness of the surrounding hills. The hushed expectancy of the massed thousands of ordinary people on the procession route, as the boom of the ancient Maligawa cannon signals the start of the procession, wed the people once again to the faith, pageantry and devotion of a bygone age.

- Vesak Nanayakkara,
A Return to Kandy, new ed. 1994.

The Perahar at Cande is ordered after this manner. The Priest bringeth forth a painted stick, about which strings of flowers are hanged, and so it is wrapped in branched Silk, some part covered, and some not; before which the people bow down and worship; each one presenting him with an offering according to his free will. These free-will offerings being received from the People, the Priest takes his painted stick on his Shoulder, having a Cloth tied about his mouth to keep his breath from defiling this pure piece of wood, and gets up upon an Elephant all covered with white cloth, upon which he rides with all the Triumph that King and Kingdom can afford, thro all the streets of the City. But before him go, first some forty or fifty Elephants, with brass Bells hanging on each side of them, which tingle as they go.

- Robert Knox,
An Historical Relation of the Island Ceylon, 1681.

Elephant

You go down shade to the river, where naked
men sit on flat brown rocks, to watch
the ferry, in the sun;
And you cross the ferry with the naked
people, go up the tropical lane
Through the palm-trees and past hollow
paddy-fields where naked men are
threshing rice
And the monolithic water-buffaloes, like old
muddy stones with hair on them, are
being idle;
And through the shadow of bread-fruit trees,
with their dark green, glossy, fanged
leaves
Very handsome, and some pure yellow fanged
leaves;
Out into the open, where the path runs on the
top of a dyke between paddy- fields;
And there of course, you meet a huge and
mud-grey elephant advancing his frontal
bone, his trunk curled round a log of
wood;
So you step down the bank, to make way.
Shuffle, shuffle, and his little wicked eye has
seen you as he advances above you,
The slow beast curiously spreading his round
feet for the dust.
And the slim naked man slips down, and the
beast deposits the lump of wood, carefully.
The keeper hooks the vast knee, the creature
salaams.
White man you are saluted.
Pay a few cents.

- D. H. Lawrence,
from *Elephant*, 1922

Kandy

Kandy

Kandy

Kandy

Kandy

Polonnaruwa

I walked through the silent halls and little grass grown cells of rooms. A brick staircase went up on my right-hand out of the main passage and ended in space. There are neither floors nor roof left today. I tried to picture those giant walls rising once again covered with plaster and rich paintings. The wooden floors were built again and bore up their couches and beds and thrones. Men of great power and lovely women walked once more in the palace, and loved, and hated, and intrigued, and thought. Out of the window I seemed to see the King's garden: "Its trees were twined about with Jasmin creepers and it was filled with the murmur of bees drunk with the enjoyment of the juice of the manifold blooms."

\- W. T. Keble,
Ceylon, Beaten Track, 1940

Embilipitiya

Seven Headed Cobra of Stone

Among these priceless treasures of our forgotten heritage is the well preserved monolithic seven headed cobra which stands over its ancient sluice in the Magam Weva (popularly known as Uru Sita Weva). The Mahaveli Authority of Sri Lanka - (Walawe Special Area), has preserved this ancient site with the concurrence of the Archaeological Department, in cordoning off the area by a well secured barbed wire fence having concrete posts. Uru Sita Weva is about six miles away from Embilipitiya on the road to Sooriya Weva.

The Seven headed cobra according to archaeological authorities, is the mythical King Cobra guarding water bodies, places of sacred worship. Such stone cobras date back to the Anuradhapura period dating from Circa 3rd Century B.C. to the 3rd century A.D.

There are some peculiar features attached to this particular sculptured seven headed cobra, quite alien to other such cobra stones found elsewhere. Around its neck is festooned a ribbon. Cobra stones placed on pedestals sculptured with seated lions, is another unique feature embodying this particular monolithic cobra.

The tip of the tail terminates on the pedestal on which there are columns of lions in relief. In the middle of the hood is etched a *punkalasa* (full vase) which issues forth flowers denoting a symbol of prosperity and plentiness.

Its *Biso-Kottuwa* which is an enclosure made of stone-slabs is in a well preserved state.

This *biso-kottuwa* is scientifically named as Valve pit. Dr. R. L. Brohier, in his *Ancient Irrigation Works in Ceylon* (Part I), defines this *Biso-Kottuwa* thus: "The works in the upstream slope of the embankment which fulfilled this most important function are termed as *Biso-Kottuwa*. Parker compares them to the 'Valve towers' and 'Valve Pits' of modern times by which the outward flow of the water in large reservoirs is regularly or totally stopped. Such being the case, the Sinhalese engineers by building these *Biso-Kottuwas* established a claim to be considered as the first inventors of the 'Valve-Pit' more than 2100 years ago".

- Gamini G. Punchihewa,
Island , 2.11.85.

VIII. A dower of the wild, the free, the beautiful

Knuckles

You ask me why I live in the grey hills and I smile but do not answer, for my thoughts are elsewhere.

- Li Po

Knuckles

Horton Plains

The lonely path, rarely trodden along which we marched, cut sometimes through the rich primaeval forest and sometimes across the wide open patenas. These are sharply distinct. The tall reed-like grasses, which are the principal growth on the patenas grow so close together, and their rhizomes form such a compact and impenetrable flooring of roots, that they fairly defy all the giants of the forest in the struggle for existence,...

- Ernst Haeckel,
A Visit to Ceylon, 1883

I had climbed the shoulder of the mountain, the path now led across flat country, springy moor,and several pretty mountain rills. Here the rhododendrons grow more luxuriantly than at home, trees three times a man's height and there is a furry, silvery plant with white blossoms, very reminiscent of the edelweiss : I found many of our familiar forest flowers but all were strangely enlarged and heightened and alpine in character. The trees here, moreover, pay no heed to timber lines but grow sturdily, with heavy foliage,right up to the greatest heights. I was approaching the last ascent of the mountain, the path suddenly began to climb again, soon I found myself once more surrounded by forest, a strange, dead, enchanted forest where trunks and branches, intertwined like serpents, stared blindly at me through long, thick, whitish beards of moss; a damp, bitter smell of foliage and fog hung between.

- Hermann Hesse, 1911

Four Things

Four things I need
To live
Complete.
Friends to share
The fragile mood;
A passionate love.
Knowledge pursued
And the luxury
Of solitude.

- Anne Ranasinghe

Talgasmankade
Mawanella

Piyadasa Lane -Yala

The fur on her belly and thighs was glistening white. Many small spots like velvet formed a bracelet round her paws; her sinuous tail was also white, ending in black rings, The back of her dress was yellow, like unburnished gold, very lissome and soft, and had the characteristic blotches in the shape of pretty rosettes, which distinguished the panther from every other species. She was three feet in height at the shoulders and four feet in length, not counting her tail; this powerful weapon was nearly three feet long and rounded like a cudgel. The head, large as that of a lioness, was distinguished by an intelligent, crafty expression. The cold cruelty of the tiger dominated, and yet it bore a vague resemblance to the face of a wanton woman.

- Honore De Balzac.
A Passion in the Desert.

◂ *Yala*

Sinharaja

The rainbow

In love one day with the beauty of evening
Happy I sat in a garden of flowers;
Birds at the time were pleasantly singing;
And I with cool winds intimate.

Rain and sunlight together appeared;
The world was a colour of festival;
Breezes came swaying the trees and branches;
But nobody else was there to be seen.

In the west the sun had set in the heavens,
Which seemed a mountain of fire at the time.
My mind was seized by a wonderful thing-
A rainbow there like a champak garland!

In colours blue, red and golden - glowing, -
Over the trees and the mountains spreading,
Tinting the world with a shower of nectar,
I saw that beautiful rainbow forming.

Not to be got at too close, but that glowing,
Colour and curve if I could but handle!
Which such a thought arose within me
Women I saw who were taking the air.

- *(Contemporary)*
tr. George Keyt. *Poetry from the Sinhalese,* 1938.

Horton Plains

I went to the woods because I wished to live deliberately, to front only the essential facts of life, and to see if I could not learn what it had to teach, and not, when I came to die, discover that I had not lived.

- Henry David Thoreau, *Walden*, 1854

Ambawela

Bibile

There is an exquisite sensibility among the leaves. They do not grow each to his own liking, till they run against one another, and then turn back sulkily; but by a watchful instinct, far apart, they anticipate their companion's courses, as ships at sea, and in every new unfolding of their edged tissue, guide themselves by the sense of each other's remote presence, and by a watchful penetration of leafy purpose in the far future. So that every shadow which one casts on the next, aid or arrest the development of their advancing form, and direct as will be safest and best, the curve of every fold and the current of every vein.

- John Ruskin,
Modern Painters, 1843-60

Maratenne

The balance of the bough of a tree is quite as subtle as that of a figure in motion. It is a balance between elasticity of the bough and the weight of leaves, affected in curvature, literally, by the growth of every leaf: and besides this, when it moves, it is partly supported by the resistance of the air, greater or less, according to the shape of the leaf; – so that branches float on the wind more than they yield to it; and in their tossing do not so much bend under a force, as rise on a wave, which penetrates in liquid threads through all their sprays.

- John Ruskin,
Modern Painters, 1843-60

Sinharaja

Ella

Thimbirimankada
Wilapalaweva

Eyelids of morning

Whose house I have made the wilderness,
And the barren land his dwelling

Job 39 : 6

Birds

from the 17 th Century Sinhala, Anonymous

Peacocks
on the craggy knolls
gaudy tail-plumes spread in
ten directions,
gloat in the sun
with
long-
drawn cries.

Ears of corn
incline like golden chaplets
and the
deep-green
parrots
with crimson beaks
clip them, and over
Alutvela
take wing, like sheaves
of rainbows.

Young swans
from the verge of the forest
emerge, flight
by flight,
like white
waves
onto land.

Here-
in Ankelihena-
restless and
greedy,
birds
everywhere – each
by its mate, at their
pleasure, feeding
on fruits and tendrils.

- Lakdasa Wikkramasinha,
Poems, 1965-1970, 1973.

Tangalle

Water-Holes

In all that great part of Ceylon where the sou'-west monsoon rains do not fall, water governs men and beasts alike, for, over hundreds of square miles, tanks and water-holes are the only places where they can drink for several months of the year. For fifteen centuries or more, each town lay beneath the bund of a large tank. And every village below a smaller one. The capital city was almost surrounded by tanks great and small, and one may infer that its position was chosen because the surrounding levels made this possible. But when prosperity swung over to the other side of the hills, the jungle tide rose over the kingdom, and age-old water-holes once more regained the importance they held between the periods of civilisation, and held for thousands of centuries before tanks existed.

- John Still,
The Jungle Tide, 1930.

Yala
Yala Block 2

The *patanas* I have briefly mentioned have always been looked upon as natural features of the hill country. Right up to their edges the forest grows unstinted, and then without, any gradual ending off in bushes or small trees, its place is taken by grass where hare-bells grow, and pink and yellow orchids. In the high hills, above five thousand feet elevation, the *patanas* are dotted with rhododendron trees in ones and tens and groves, not close generally, but spaced like the trees in an abandoned orchard; and the sight of a group of these, radiant with crimson blossom, makes one stop and take a deep breath in the half-conscious effort to absorb the whole joy of such unrivalled beauty. Lower down another tree, the *kahata*, takes the rhododendron's place in the *patanas*.

- John Still,
The Jungle Tide, 1930.

Horton Plains

Horton Plains

Handapanagala

Ode to elephant

Gross innocent,
Saint Elephant,
blessed beast
of the perduring forests,
bulk of our palpable world
in its counterpoise,
mighty
and exquisite,
a saddlery's cosmos
in leather,
ivory
packed into satins
unmoved
like
the flesh of the moon,
minimal eyes
to observe, without being observed,
horn
virtuoso
and bugling
propinquity,
animal
waterspout
elate
in
its
cleanliness,
portable
engine
and telephone booth in a forest:
so
softly you go
in your swagger,
with your ageing caparison
in the wrinkle and pile
of a tree's regimentals,
your pants
at your ankles,
trailing your tail-end.

Make no mistake:
that endeared and enormous
sojourner of jungles is nobody's clown;
he is patriarch,
father of emerald lights,
the ancient
and innocent
sire of the universe.

All the fruits of earth,
and the longings
of Tantalus,
the multitudinous
skin
and the ways of
the rain
have encompassed
the kingdom of
elephants;
with brine
and
with blood
they accomplished the war
of their species in silence.

The scale-bearing kind,
the lizards-turned-lion,
the fish in the mountains
and gargantuan ground sloth
succumbed
and decayed:
they
leavened the green of the bog,
a prize
for the sweltering fly
and the scarab's barbarity.
But the elephant rose
on the wreck of his fears -
almost a vegetable, a shadowy pylon
in his emerald heaven,
to suckle his young
on the sweet of the leaves, and the water
and honey of stones...

- Pablo Neruda,
Selected Poems, 1961.

Neruda regarded as Latin America's finest and most prolific poet was awarded the Nobel Prize for Literature in 1971. He died two years later of cancer at the age of sixty nine. He worked for his government in consular positions in Asia from 1927 to 1932,and at the age of 24 was Consul in Ceylon from 1929 to 1930. He lived in a seaside house in Wellawatte identified as No. 56, 42nd Lane, and became involved in the literary and artistic circle in which Lionel Wendt, George Keyt and Charles Winzer moved. Both the idyllic beauty and the gentle character of its people were to leave an indelible mark of nostalgia in his poetry and prose. His residence in the island influenced several poems he wrote in this and later periods, and are specifically redolent of his special feel for the island and its environment. He returned only once in 1957 to Ceylon.

- H. A. I. Goonetileke

Udawalawe

Yala

Udawalawe

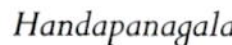

Handapanagala

Eye of a dying elephant - Sella Kataragama

There was no sound; he gave no cry,
The careless stars looked on serene.
The jungles sudden tragedy
Remained unheard, unknown, unseen.
- Lawrence Hope

Extracts from a letter attributed (whether rightly or wrongly is of no importance) to the American Indian chief Seattle, chief of the Dwamish, Suquamish and allied Indian tribes. The letter, apparently written with the help of an amanuensis, is believed to have been sent in 1854 to President Franklin Pierce, following the request by the US government to acquire their tribal lands.

"How can you buy or sell the sky, the warmth of the land? The idea is strange to us. If we do not own the freshness of the air and the sparkle of the water, how can you buy them? Every part of this earth is sacred to my people.

Every shining pine needle, every sandy shore, every mist in the dark woods, every clearing and humming insect is holy in the memory and experience of my people. The sap which courses through the trees carries the memories of the red man.

The white man's dead forget the country of their birth when they go to walk among the stars. Our dead never forget this beautiful earth, for it is the mother of the red man.

We are part of the earth and it is part of us. The perfumed flowers are our sisters; the deer, the horse, the great eagle, these are our brothers. The rocky crests, the juices in the meadows, the body heat of the pony and man – all belong to the same family...

This shining water that moves in the streams and rivers is not just water but the blood of our ancestors ... The rivers are our brothers, they quench our thirst...

We know that the white man does not understand our ways. One portion of land is the same to him as the next, for he is a stranger who comes in the night and takes from the land whatever he needs. The earth is not his brother but his enemy, and when he has conquered it, he moves on. He leaves his father's graves behind, and he does not care...

His father's grave and his children's birthright, are forgotten. He treats his mother, the earth, and his brother the sky, as things to be bought, plundered, sold like sheep or bright beads. His appetite will devour the earth and leave behind only a desert...

What is man without the beasts? If all the beasts were gone, man would die from a great loneliness of spirit. For whatever happens to the beasts, soon happens to man. All things are connected...

Whatever befalls the earth befalls the sons of the earth... Man did not weave the web of life, he is merely a strand in it. Whatever he does to the web, he does to himself."

-*The Faber Book of Letters*;
ed. F. Pryor, London, Faber, 1988.

Block 2 Yala

Jamburagala

The Green Pigeon

O flutterer of green, amid green leaves,
Is it joy, pure joy, makes you whistle like a boy,
Knowing half a tune he never quite achieves?

O Learner of a wistful melody,
I can hear your quaint refrain, lilting down and up again,
Where you crouch among the leaves half-hid from me.

O Teacher of a woodland harmony,
I can see your colours blend with the leaves, and without end
Through my heart there runs the tune you taught to me.

- John Still,
The Jungle Tide, 1930

Siyambalagaswela

Wild buffaloes on bended knees drag their hoofs,
Rearing high their head and hunch with ears erect;
They utter loud a guttural growl then spring aside
And join in strife, horn to horn, far and near.

- *Maga Salakuna;* tr. Edmund Peiris and M. E. Fernando, 1947.

If any desire to know how this white Deer was caught, it was thus; This Deer was observed to come on Evenings with the rest of the Herd to a great Pond to drink; the People that were ordered to catch this Deer, fenced the Pond round and plain about it with high stakes, leaving, only one wide gap. The men after this done lay in ambush, each with his bundle of Stakes ready cut. In the Evening the Deer came with the rest of the Herd to drink according to their wont. As soon as they were entred within the stakes, the men in ambush fell to their work, which was to fence in the gap left, which there being little less than a Thousand men, they soon did; and so all the Herd were easily caught; and this among the rest.

- Robert Knox, 1681.

Wilpattu

Udawalawe

Initiation

(First Flight)

(From '*Sinhala Daruva,*'1938. [*Kiyavana Nuvana*]

Why is the morning sun today
Up so soon and on his way?
'Sunbeams! Let each darting ray
Haste me to the bird - home gay.'

What happy hour approaches there?
'The fledgelings wait to brave the air
And for my coming all's set fair,
To hurry on is now my care.'

- Munidasa Kumaranatunga,
Verses 1-2,
Translated by Gamini Salgado
- An Anthology of Sinhalese Literature of the Twentieth Century, 1987

Wasgamuwa

The breeding season is not well defined. A cow in heat makes certain subdued noises to attract the male and the pair keep together for about a week. Copulation occurs at all seasons. The male places his chin upon the female's hips and steadying himself with his trunk and tusks or tushes placed on either side of her verterbral ridge he raises himself on to her back and places a fore foot on either side of her spine. Bringing his hind legs closer to the female he assumes a squatting posture and raises his head off her back, next the fully extended penis curves upwards, and after a series of horizontal as well as vertical movements effects entry. He then straightens his hind legs and assumes an almost erect posture.

Udawalawe

Udawalawe

If the cow is much smaller than the bull she may drop on to her bent fore legs under his weight. Copulation barely lasts a minute but may be repeated at frequent intervals for several days. Many erroneous ideas exist about this, and it is a popular fallacy that elephants are very retiring in their mating habits and will not copulate if human beings are present.

There are many instances of wild elephants driven into a stockade or kraal and surrounded by several thousands of people, mating after their terror subsided. A recent example was at the Panamure Kraal of November 1950, when the large herd leader mated freely with a cow which gave birth to a male calf 21 months later.

P.E.P. Deraniyagala,
Some Extinct Elephants,
their relatives and the two living species, 1955.

Udawalawe

Udawalawe

Gonagala -Yala
Udawalawe

Here is a sort of Bird they call Carlo, which never lighteth on the ground, but always sets on very high Trees. He is as big as a Swan, the colour black, the Legs very short, the Head monstrous, his Bill very long, a little rounding like a Hawks, and white on each side of the head like ears: on the top of the crown groweth out a white thing, somewhat like to the comb of a cock : commonly they keep four or five of them together and always are hopping from bough to bough. They are seldom silent, but continually make a roaring noise, somewhat like the quacking of a Duck, that they may be heard at least a mile off; the reason they thus cry, the Chingulayes say, is for Rain, that they may drink. The bodies of these Fowls are good to eat.

\- Robert Knox 1681

Thimbirimankade

Here are other sorts of small Birds, not much bigger than a Sparrow, very lovely to look on, but I think good for nothing else; some being in colour white like snow and their tail about one foot in length, and their heads black like jet, with a tuft like a plume of Feathers standing upright thereon. There are others of the same sort only differing in colour, being reddish like a ripe Orange, and on the head a Plume of black feathers standing up. I suppose one may be the cock and the other the Hen.

- Robert Knox, 1681

An evening in Bundala; through the plains and thorny forest we travelled, chasing the dying sun, and the flights of ibis that crossed the horizon.

As the light hid behind clouds and painted them red and gold, we reached the bund of the lewaya, a broad lagoon that sheltered Bundala's most familiar and yet ever elusive inhabitant the Greater Flamingo.

The *Lewaya* stretched out before us - a landscape in miniature : a lake, a desert, clothed in salt and sand, and shallow water. The blue, a bright contrast against the grey mud and the fringe of green cactus that surrounded it all.

Our flamingos were there too, in a loose gathering of two flocks, feeding ankle-deep, with their heads held low and their down-turned beaks dining, filter-like; sieving the water for their minute, crustacean reward. Displaying occasionally, re-working the ancient, ritualised imitations of everyday life - wing saluting, head bowing and preening. A hundred, perhaps more individuals moving as one, back and forth in unison and rhythmic cohesion.

In the centre of their blue stage, they danced; pink fading to white and the crimson streak that tipped their wings. We watched at a distance, and filled our lenses with their merging colours and shapes.

And so it was with momentary disbelief and even greater delight that we saw, close to the lapping, receding waters, standing like abandoned castles of sand - a colony on nest platforms. The unique, incubating mounds of mineral and mud, that cradle the eggs and serve as a refuge for the young in the first days of their lives.

Six hundred and thirty five in all, some eight inches, some as high as one and a half feet. In varying conditions, with the onset of age and passing seasons, but their purpose was all too apparent. The tantalising glimpse of a feather close - by; further evidence of their intimate link with the dancers in the distance.

There have never been recorded sightings of breeding flamingos or their chicks in our island. Migratory, they arrive from land uncertain and leave without trace. It is an age-old cycle, but now we have evidence, however open to speculation it may be, that the flamingos have come with an intention to breed. They have prepared their nesting grounds and await their opportunity.

What remains to be seen is whether we will allow them to follow their natural rhythms. Evidence of our ever-threatening ignorance lay in two deep tyre tracks, driven straight through a group of mounds. All destroyed, apart from one - tall and intact. A message of how it is and how it could be. Preserve or destroy. As in the case of the ghost elephants that move silently within the surrounding scrub, and the langurs that bark in the nearby trees; and in all of us who walk, swim or fly. The instinctive urge to create, to raise young. To live in our children. Flamingos never return to a disturbed nest site - the threat of predator interference is too great. But in other areas they will try, and during the course of their fifty-year life span and with their life-long partners, they will try again. Who are we to stand in their way?

Flamingos - the Portuguese knew them as flamebirds. And cultures older still, like the Egyptians knew them too, and respected their mysterious place in nature's order. And they built a legend around their lives, and gave them a name. Phoenix. The sacred bird that rose out of the ashes of desolation and disappeared into nowhere. And never returned.

- Charith Pelpola, 1997.

Gilimale

Handapanagala

Journey

I discovered solitude on the hills
the language of silence among the roots of earth
above me walking into its own stillness
steps of hills climbed reaching into a sky
stripped clear of feather clouds
the moulting bird of childhood's seasons
no wound to practise pain rehearsed the
flight that winged me through the leafy
branches crowded with bird and fruit
on the high rock where agile goats leaped wild
myself shut in within the hard green pod
yet to be seared by sun
curled round its seed, tight in the teeth of core.

- Jean Arasanayagam,
A Colonial Inheritance and other poems, 1985, verse 1

Gilimale

If it were a question of defending rivers, hills, mountains, skies, winds, rains, I would say, 'Willingly. That is our job. Let us fight. All our happiness in life is there.' No, we have defended the sham name of all that.

\- Jean Giono.

The wilderness of only half a century ago, then so completely itself, has been reduced, tree by tree, animal by animal, shadow by shadow, rock by rock, to its last rutted corners. The few remaining spaces have been infiltrated, divided-up, domesticated, deprived of natural systems, denuded of natural processes, systematized, similarized, artificialized, sterilized, commercialized . . .

\- Peter Beard,
End of the Game, The Last Word From Paradise, 1988.

Gondaviddagala

Kalawewa

Kalawewa

The highest wisdom has but one science - the science of the whole - the science explaining the whole creation and man's place in it.

- Jonathan Scott,
Kingdom of the Lions, 1992.

Surely it is obvious enough, if one looks at the whole world that it is becoming daily better cultivated and more fully peopled. All places are now accessible, all are well known; most pleasant farms have obliterated all traces of what were once dreary and dangerous wastes; cultivated fields and subdued forests, flocks and herds have expelled wild beasts; sandy deserts are sown; rocks are planted; marshes are drained; and where once were hardly solitary cottages, there are now large cities. No longer are islands dreaded, nor their rocky shores feared; everywhere are houses and inhabitants. Our teeming population is the strongest evidence: our numbers are burdensome to the world which can hardly supply us from its natural elements; our wants grow more and more keen, and our complaints more bitter in all mouths, whilst Nature fails in affording us her usual sustenance. In every deed, pestilence, and famine and wars, and earthquakes have to be regarded as a remedy for nations, as the means of pruning the luxuriance of the human race.

- Tertullian 337 A.D.
Peter Beard,
End of the Game, The Last Word From Paradise, 1988.

Samanalawewa

Nildandahinna

We live in an old chaos of the sun,
Or old dependency of day and night,
Or island solitude, unsponsored, free,
Of that wide water, inescapable.
Deer walk upon our mountains, and the quail
Whistle about us their spontaneous cries;
Sweet berries ripen in the wilderness;
And, in the isolation of the sky,
At evening, casual flocks of pigeons make
Ambiguous undulations as they sink
Downward to darkness, on extended wings.

- Wallace Stevens

Seven Virgins Forest

Knuckles

Who can answer a riddle?
A riddle sir, ask me sir.
A hard one sir?
This is the riddle:
'When that which drew
from out the boundless
deep, turns again home'
- Again sir. We didn't hear.
(riddle repeated)
- what is it sir?
- We give it up.
A turtle scuttling back
seaward, its eggs laid.

Does she make it? No of course not. But not a few hatchlings do. Escaping nature's 'tooth and claw' – ghost-crabs, gulls, sea eagles, sharks, they reach mid-ocean. And, sorry not to be able to chime in with the romantic folklorists and the Greens, year after year they keep coming back in force to Lanka's beaches, mated and ready to spawn. Some inlaid magnetic magic guides them here perhaps. But each to a natal beach? Doubtful. And that's the disenchanting long and short of that.

Now for the mothers, their task completed, struggling to get back to water. On every golden or moonlit strand South East to South West to North, they fall prey not just to Nature but human nature in this case. Turned turtle, as the infamous phrase has it, they are vivisected piece-meal till only the beautifully mottled and cloudy shells remain, the prize of so much barbarity. Christians, Hindus and yes, Buddhists, do it. The fisherfolk and the non-fishers do it. Even the little black tortoises of the paddies don't go scot free. So if you have tears to spare, shed some for these gentle, sad-eyed creatures so unconscionably forced to be so long a time a-dying. And if tears are scarce in this land of the Compassionate One, crocodile like just cry fie for shame.

- Robert Silva, 1996.

Kosgoda

Albino Turtle - Kosgoda

Hoom-mane - Kudawella

Yala - Block 2

Blow-holes are rare freaks of nature. They occur in association with the sea coast, where a naturally occurring rock tunnel leading inwards from the water's edge ends up in a vertical direction among the rocky formations. They have a large opening like a small cavern at the sea end, and a much smaller orifice at the vertical end. Due to the action of the sea waves, large amounts of water get ejected out with great force to produce a spectacular fountain reaching great heights.

Only six or seven blow-holes are known to exist in the entire world, and Sri Lanka is lucky to possess the second largest of them all. It is astonishing that these are so few in number considering the vast extent of coastlines in the world.

Hoom-mane as it is known locally is situated in a little village off Mawella about 183 kms. down the A2 trunk road. A sign board indicates the turn-off to the right. The road is motorable upto a point and is signposted. The vehicle will have to be parked in a private compound, from where is a short walk up two hillocks to the summit where the blow-hole is situated.

- A.N. Dharmawansa, *Loris* 20 (6), Dec. 1995.

Kudremalai

The traditional occupation of this area dates back to antiquity, even before the legendary landing of Wijaya (circa 600 B.C). Kudremalai or Horse Mountain makes reference to the horse. The horse was traditionally associated with the Persians, Arabs, who imported them to Sri Lanka in their sailing ships from the Persian Gulf as well as the Greeks, (one is reminded here of the Trojan horse in Greek mythology). We see the ruins of an ancient monument, that of a rearing Horse of enormous height, nearly 35ft. tall, facing the sea at Kudremalai Point. This indicates its association with Hippuros, the name of the ancient sea port referred to by former foreign writers of Sri Lanka. According to Hugh Nevill in his *Taprobanian*, Acha Nagara is Horse city. The horse also no doubt was a prominent landmark that gave identity to this area.

- R. L. Brohier,
The Golden Plains, 1923, *Notes of Topographic Survey of the ancient coastal habitations between Puttalam and Mannar and subsequent observations.*
Edited by Deloraine Brohier, 1992.

Beragala

In the forest, far behind,
Came a crash as the passing wind
Gave touch to death, and a King who stood,
Came thundering down, and lay, but wood,
With his crown the wreath that the sorrowing
orchids bind.

\- John Still,
1925, *New Ceylon Writing*, 4, 1979.

. . . All over the world mountains and hillsides are being denuded of forest as more land is brought under cultivation. The forest used to bind the soil together, shield it from the heat of the sun, and act as a sponge which slowly released water bit by bit throughout the year. With the forest gone the springs coming out of the hillsides stop, catching the land in the vicious circle of flood and drought. The rains rush down the slopes, taking the precious top soil with them. It is not long before the resulting erosion changes a once fertile hillside into a desert, leaving only the rocks resembling a carcass devoured by scavengers and the bones left in the sun to bleach.

Whenever man has meddled with the balance of nature the results have been disastrous. When will we learn? If we abuse nature we will have to pay, one day. Pollution of the air, the sea, overpopulation, destruction of our habitat these are all cheques drawn on the future. For centuries we have lived on the capital nature provided us with. Decades ago we used it up; now all the cheques increase the overdraft. One day we shall have to pay whether we like it or not.

You may ask what all this has got to do with wildlife; and if there are all these pressing problems why worry about wilderness areas and national parks?

Wildlife reserves and wilderness areas are our only visible remaining link with true nature. Managed and protected, they are among the few inexhaustible resources a country can have. In the future, as more and more of these areas fall to the axe and the plough, this will be even more true. True wild places provide us with a connection to our heritage. If we destroy that connection we shall drift about aimlessly, like orphans looking for the parents they never knew.

- Dieter Plage,
Wild Horizons, A Cameraman in Africa, 1980.

Balagoda - Haputale

IX. Serendip. A lost paradise?

SERENDIP
Dom Moraes

Prologue

The first man's footstep
Is stone on a hilltop.
The dead king's tooth,
Held steady in stone,
Is bereft of its body,
Now a forest stone
Celebrated on stone,
The brushwork is blurred
In the mountain cave
Of hibiscus and wasp,
But dead king, first man,
Though frozen to frieze
As they start the dance,
Retain a relevance.

(I)
The privileged foot rests
On the stone peak, forests
Under; the knotted sea,
A chequered net, beyond.
Dolphins trying to escape
Leap, but, stunned by sun.
Drop back to the clouded
Depths where sundered ships
Wallow in the powdery shrouds.
Currents sift dead crews,
Lift the bones of a hand.
The luminous eyes look
Down from the stone peak
Of the unattained island.

(II)
Jungles where geometric shapes
Cease to exist; dry riverbeds
Cratered like the moon, strewn
With expended stones; slopes
Of stone; skeletal
Ridges of stone. Anthill menhirs
Chart the runestones of the moon
Timekeeper of the tides,
Home of the hare, and those
Taught to obey the leaves.
Under stone and helianthus

Are the ossuaries of the fathers.
Gnawed by the sea, the silent
Island awaits visitors.

(III)
From ships beached on stone,
Bleached exiles, faces etched
By firewind, fetched their lives.
Language formed on the lip.
They settled, they bred,
Watched by eyes of the forest,
Shy behind helianthus.
They evolved codes of conduct.
With the wheel and the tool
They composed a culture:
Symbols scratched on stone
Hewn to build temples.
Thing, place, creature,
Named, therefore known.

(IV)
Jewels prised from stone,
Pools of blood in the palm:
Predator's bait. Elara's
Slow drums beat offshore.
Uncalm water saw boats
Sundered in seawrack; stone,
Bonecrack, blood under blade.
Six months, then the kings met.
Under trees they discussed music,
Not forgetting the allied arts,
In speech broken by silence
Within which was the word.
Not a bird spoke as they heard
Its proclamation of peace.

(V)
Every breath off the island
Reeks of putrescent spice,
Disseminated by winds
Troubled by constant sails.
Under, in tousled beds,
Are oysters heavy with pearl,
Phosphorescent eels, singing fish.
Beggars have ridden wishes
To the island of sirens.
South, the Sinhala; northward,
Angry descendants of Elara.
In the forest, the survivors:
Luminous eyes sealed by leaves,
Footsteps no longer privileged.

(VI)
Ichor of the incised trees;
Beverages packed in containers
By sullen descendants of Elara;
Processions of ivory elephants
In diminishing sizes, birthstones
In brooches; spices in bottles.
All these, sent beyond the sun
To be unshipped on cold quays
Of another island. Where deer leapt,
Where panther stepped; no forest.
Where pilgrims with lamps went
No passage left a mark:
Only the smell of pasts
Locked in a keyless dark.

(VII)
Parliament for an island
Bewildered with new flags.
Old grudges, latent for years,
Were nudged to hate in the north.
Components, hidden under stone,
Lodged in stodgy armalite,
Were assembled, iridescent
Compounds packed in containers
By a local complex; the cottage
Industry soon went national,
With different target audiences.
Some applauded the event;
But the unforeseen nature
Of the product shook parliament.

(VIII)
The revolutions of the island
Sent it beyond the sun,
Requiring emended horoscopes.
The shy child whom the explosion
Taught to fly, needed none.
The pensioners and their wives
Gave their lives up meekly
To grenade and to gun.
So with the other corpses,
More or less tidily disposed of,
Though not by name or profession:
Only remembered as numbers
In files that would be cremated
When their brief day was done.

Epilogue
Perhaps an evening waits
Beyond the ruptured bridge
Of some wrecked village, where
Pilgrims with lamps resume,
From memory, the trek.
Perhaps a night will come
When the luminous eyes return
To the summit of the peak:
When the privileged foot stamps
To a dance beyond drums.
Stone of the lamps, reborn,
Will shine from within stone,
If such an evening waits,
If such a night should come.

Dom Moraes was born in Bombay in 1938 as an only child, and indulged a voracious passion for reading and a precocious gift for writing from an early age. Before he was fifteen he had seen most parts of emerging Asia. The first of his journeys began when he was eight, when his father Frank Moraes was appointed Editor of the *Times of Ceylon*. He spent two years in Colombo travelling incessantly throughout the country to quell his feelings of loneliness. This piece of anguished childhood is dealt with at length in his autobiography *My Son's Father* (1968). But Ceylon remained a rhapsodic memory even after he returned to lead his own life as poet and man of letters. His first book of poems *A Beginning* published when he was an Oxford undergraduate of nineteen won him the Hawthornden Prize, the youngest writer ever to have won this prestigious award. He now lives in Bombay, and his *Collected Poems 1957-1987* was published by Penguin Books in 1987. His interest in Sri Lanka never faded, and the communal convulsions of July 1983 affected him greatly. The poem sequence "Serendip" appeared on the sixth anniversary of the carnage, in the *Illustrated Weekly of India*. It was reprinted in *The Island*, 17 December, 1989.

In a poignantly metaphorical sense, the poem is an epitome of the book in its ten stanzas. It encapsulates the historical sequence of events from the legendary footprint on the Sacred Peak, to the coming of the Indian colonizer, the beginnings of civilization and its epic forms, external invasions, internal strife, the advent of the white man, mercantilism and modernity, the clash of cultures, and hopeful transfiguration in the end.

- H.A.I. Goonetileke

X. The sound of the sea

The Sea of Faith
Was once, too, at the full and round earth's
 shore
Lay like the folds of a bright girdle furled.
But now I only hear
Its melancholy, long, withdrawing roar,
Retreating, to the breath
Of the night-wind, down the vast edges drear
And naked shingles of the world.
- Matthew Arnold, from : *Dover Beach*

For tho' from out our bourne
of Time and Place
The flood may bear me far,
I hope to see my Pilot face to face
When I have crost the bar.
- Alfred, Lord Tennyson. *Crossing the Bar*

The moon too sheds not her soft beams
All at once in thick cascades
But strains through clouds in gentle streams
And a soft and restful glow pervades.
- Folk Poem, Munidasa Kumaranatunga,
Lullaby. Translated by Hemamali Gunasinghe.

The Fisherman Mourned by His Wife

When you were not quite thirty and the sun
Had not yet tanned you into old-boat brown,
When you were not quite thirty and had not
begun
To be embittered like the rest, nor grown
Obsessed with death, then would you come
Hot with continence upon the sea
Chaste as a gull flying pointed home,
In haste to be with me!

Now that, being dead, you are beyond detection,
And I need not be discreet, let us confess
It was not love that married us nor affection,
But elders' persuasion, not even loneliness.
Recall how first you were so impatient and
afraid,
My eyes were open in the dark unlike in love,
Trembling, lest in fear, you'll let me go a maid,
Trembling on the other hand, for my virginity.

Three months the monsoon thrashed the sea,
and you
Remained at home; the sky cracked like a shell
In thunder, and the rain broke through.
At last when pouring ceased and storm winds
fell,
When gulls returned new-plumed and wild,
When in our wind-torn flamboyante
New buds broke, I was with child.

My face was wan while telling you and voice
fell low,
And you seemed full of guilt and not to know
Whether to repent or rejoice over the situation.
You nodded at the ground and went to sea.
But soon I was to you more than God or
temptation,
And so were you to me.
Men come and go, some say they understand,
Our children weep, the youngest thinks
you're fast asleep:
Theirs is fear and wonderment.
You had grown so familiar as my hand,

That I cannot with simple grief
Assuage dismemberment.
Outside the wind despoils of leaf
Trees that it used to nurse;
Once more the flamboyante is torn,
The sky cracks like a shell again,
So someone practical has gone
To make them bring the hearse
Before the rain.

- Patrick Fernando, *Selected Poems,* 1984.

Many gods and many voices.
The salt is on the briar rose,
The fog is in the fir trees.
The sea howl
And the sea yelp, are different voices
Often together heard: the whine in the rigging,
The menace and caress of wave that breaks on water,
The distant rote in the granite teeth,
And the wailing warning from the approaching headland
Are all sea voices, and the heaving groaner
Rounded homewards, and the seagull:
And under the oppression of the silent fog
The tolling bell
Measures time not our time, rung by the unhurried
Ground swell, a time
Older than the time of chronometers, older
Than time counted by anxious worried women
Lying awake, calculating the future,
Trying to unweave, unwind, unravel,
And piece together the past and the future,
Between midnight and dawn, when the past is all deception,
The future futureless, before the morning watch
When time stops and time is never ending;
And the ground swell, that is and was from the beginning,
Clangs
The bell.

\- T. S. Eliot, *The Dry Salvages*, 1941

As the dissolving warmth of dawn may fold
A half unfrozen dew-globe, green, and gold,
And crystalline, till it becomes a winged mist,
And wanders up the vault of the blue day,
Outlives the noon, and on the sun's last ray
Hangs o'er the sea, a fleece of fire and
amethyst.

- Percy Bysshe Shelley

There is a society where none intrudes
By the deep sea, and the music of its roar.

- Byron

The river is within us, the sea is all about us;
The sea is the land's edge also, the granite
Into which it reaches, the beaches where it tosses
Its hints of earlier and other creation:
The starfish, the hermit crab, the whale's
backbone;
The pools where it offers to our curiosity
The more delicate algae and the sea anemone.
It tosses up our losses, the torn seine,
The shattered lobsterpot, the broken oar
And the gear of foreign dead men. The sea has
many voices.

- T. S. Eliot, *The Dry Salvages,* 1941

We thank with brief thanksgiving
Whatever gods may be,
That no man lives forever
That dead men rise up never;
That even the weariest river
Winds somewhere safe to sea.
- A. C. Swinburne. *The Garden of Proserpine*

The Sea

I need an ocean to teach me:
whatever it is that I learn – music or
consciousness,
the single wave in the sea, the abyss of my being,
the guttural rasp of my voice, or the blazing
presumption of fishes and navies –
so much is certain: even in sleep, as if
by the trick of a magnet, I spin on the circle
of wave upon wave of the sea, the sea's university.

More than the mash of the sea-conch, as though
worn by a planet's vibrations that dies by degrees,
I salvage the day with a fragment,
restore the stalactite with a volley of salt
and spoon up a godhead's immensity.

And all that I learn is remembered. It is air,
it is sand, it is water, the interminable wind.

The young think it little,
coming to live here with their fires;
yet out of those recesses where a pulse once
ascended or sank to its void,
the crackle and freeze of the blue,
a star's granulation,
the tender deployment of waves
that squander their snow on the foam,
the reticent power, undeflectable,
a stone throne on the deep,
my wayward despondency, heaping oblivion
higher,
turned, until suddenly all my existence was
changed:

and I cling with the whole of my being to what
is purest in movement.

- Pablo Neruda,
A New Decade : Poems 1958-1967, 1969

When were the winds
Let slip with such a warrant to destroy?
When did the waves so haughtily overleap
Their ancient barriers?

- Frank Modder,
Manual of the Puttalam District, 1908.

Old men ought to be explorers
Here and there does not matter
We must be still and still moving
Into another intensity
For a further union, a deeper communion
Through the dark cold and the empty
desolation,
The wave cry, the wind cry, the vast waters
Of the petrel and the porpoise. In my end is
my beginning.

- T. S. Eliot, *East Coker,* 1944.

Sea Fever

I must down to the seas again,
to the lonely sea and the sky,
And all I ask is a tall ship and a
star to steer her by,
And the wheel's kick and the
wind's song and the white sails showing,
And a grey mist on the sea's face
and a grey dawn breaking
I must down to the sea again,
for the call of the running tide
Is a wild call and a clear call that
may not be denied.

- John Masefield.

Magna Est Veritas

Here, in this little Bay,
Full of tumultuous life and great repose,
Where, twice a day,
The purposeless, glad ocean
comes and goes,
Under high cliffs, and far from
the huge town,
I sit me down.
For want of me the world's
course will not fail:
When all its work is done, the lie shall rot;
The truth is great, and shall prevail,
When none cares whether it prevail or not.

- Coventry Patmore (1823 - 1896)

Soliloquy in the waves

Yes, but it's lonely here.
The wave builds
and breaks, speaking
its name, it may be: I understand nothing.
A murmur arises, dragging its weight
in the foam and flotation,
falls back again. Who's to say
what it says to me there?
Whom shall I call
from the wave?
I wait.

Another time, clarity
falls very close: the sweet number
heaves up in the spray
but I cannot decipher it.
Like a sigh moving down from the air:
a slithering mouth in the sand:
time wrecks all the lips
with the patience
of darkness, the
tangerine kiss
of the summer.
Bereft and alone,
I go numb to the manifest
grace of the world,
hearing
some bounty that batters itself into bits,
mysterious grapes
in the salt, love undisclosed;
until only a rumour
remains of the day's degradation,
each moment more distant,
and the imminent gift of the possible
turns wholly toward silence.

- Pablo Neruda, *A New Decade : Poems 1958-1967*, 1969

The tides

Drenched in my natural waters, I came of age
like the mollusk in nautical phosphor;
salts broke and rebounded in me,
contrived the device of my intimate skeleton.
How give it a name – something almost
unmoved in itself, in the blue, bitter breathing
that gave back to me, wave after wave,
my unique intimations; that seethed
and then bodied me forth in the brine and the
resin:
the disdain and desire of a wave,
green rhythm at the heart of a mystery
that raised a diaphanous mansion;
a secret reserved to itself that I later
sensed as my own, like a pulse beat made
mine,
till my song came of age, with the water.

- Pablo Neruda,
A New Decade : Poems 1958-1967, 1969

Farewell

When I lie where shades of darkness
Shall no more assail mine eyes,
Nor the rain make lamentation
  When the wind sighs;
How will fare the world whose wonder
Was the very proof of me?
Memory fades, must the remembered
  Perishing be?

Oh, when this my dust surrenders
Hand, foot, lip, to dust again,
May these loved and loving faces
  Please other men!
May the rusting harvest hedgerow
Still the Traveller's Joy entwine,
And as happy children gather
  Posies once mine.

Look thy last on all things lovely,
Every hour. Let no night
Seal thy sense in deathly slumber
  Till to delight
Thou have paid thy utmost blessing;
Since that all things thou wouldst praise
Beauty took from those who loved them
  In other days.

- Walter De La Mare, *Motley*, 1918

When you are old

When you are old and gray and full of sleep
And nodding by the fire, take down this book,
And slowly read, and dream of the soft look
Your eyes had once, and of their shadows deep;

How many loved your moments of glad grace,
And loved your beauty with love false or true;
But one man loved the pilgrim soul in you,
And loved the sorrows of your changing face.

And bending down beside the glowing bars
Murmur, a little sadly, how love fled
And paced upon the mountains overhead,
And hid his face amid a crowd of stars.

- William Butler Yeats, 1892.